The Australian Women's Weekly — Home Library

Oriental Dinner Party COOKBOOK

EDITOR: Maryanne Blacker

FOOD EDITOR: Pamela Clark

DESIGN DIRECTOR: Neil Carlyle

• • •

DESIGNER: Robbylee Phelan

• • •

ASSISTANT FOOD EDITOR:
Barbara Northwood

HOME ECONOMISTS: Lucy Clayton,
Wendy Berecry, Jo-anne Power, Sue Hipwell

PHOTOGRAPHERS: Ashley Mackevicius,
Robert Mort

EDITORIAL ASSISTANT: Evelyn Follers

KITCHEN ASSISTANT: Amy Wong

• • •

HOME LIBRARY STAFF:

ASSISTANT EDITOR: Judy Newman

DESIGNER: Paula Wooller

EDITORIAL CO-ORDINATOR: Sanchia Roth

• • •

PUBLISHER: Richard Walsh

DEPUTY PUBLISHER: Graham Lawrence

ASSOCIATE PUBLISHER: Bob Neil

• • •

Produced by The Australian Women's Weekly
Home Library Division
Typeset by Photoset Computer Service Pty Ltd,
and Letter Perfect, Sydney. Printed by Dai Nippon Co Ltd,
Tokyo, Japan. Published by Australian Consolidated Press,
54 Park Street Sydney. Distributed by Network Distribution
Company, 54 Park Street Sydney. Distributed in the U.K. by
Australian Consolidated Press (UK) Ltd (0604) 760 456.
Distributed in New Zealand by Netlink Distribution
Company (9) 302 7616 . Distributed in Canada by Whitecap
Books Ltd (604) 980 9852. Distributed in South Africa by
Intermag (011) 493 3200.

• • •

Oriental Dinner Party Cookbook

Includes index.

ISBN 0 949128 75 9

1. Cookery, Oriental. (Series: Australian
Women's Weekly Home Library).

641.595

• • •

• • •

Wonderfully flavoursome Oriental cooking has gained enormous popularity in Australia; we've brought together exciting S.E. Asian cuisines in planned menus for all occasions. Even the great Australian barbecue has a spicy new twist! We decided to adapt certain specialities, spices and ingredients to suit Australian tastes and lifestyles. All recipes are pictured, many with step-by-step directions. Some do-ahead, microwave and freezing tips are included. Ingredients are explained and substitutes given where possible in the Glossary. All ingredients we suggest are readily available in specialised Asian food supply stores.

Pamela Clark

FOOD EDITOR

FRONT COVER: Thailand: Marinated Herbed Quail with Carrot Salad; China: Scallops with Coriander; India: Masala Lamb; Japan: Sushi. BACK COVER: Vietnam: Beef and Bean Sprouts with Noodles; China: Seafood and Vegetables on Lettuce; Korea: Crispy Sesame Prawns with Pickled Cabbage; Indonesia: Spicy Mixed Satays; Malaysia: Chilli Sweet Lobster with Compressed Ginger Rice.
OPPOSITE: Back, from left: Snow White Strawberry Jelly, Orange Jelly Mousse, Lychee Mousse; centre: Mixed Melon and Ginger Fruit Salad; front: Moist Coconut Pie.
COVER CREDITS: Background Regimental Red laminate by Wilsonart from Parbury Henty Gibbs Bright Pty. Ltd, Sydney; Vietnam: Blue Siam plates from Wedgwood; Korea: Sasaki plate from Dansab Pty. Ltd, Chippendale, NSW; Japan: plates from Made in Japan, Neutral Bay, NSW; Malaysia: Taitu plate from Lifestyle Imports, Chippendale, NSW. OPPOSITE CREDITS: Screen from Ukiyo-No, Annandale, NSW; table and stand from Chin Hua Galleries, Crows Nest, NSW; teapot is Lunar by Wedgwood; teacups from Made in Japan, Neutral Bay, NSW; plates are Sasaki from Dansab Pty. Ltd, Chippendale, NSW.

BRITISH & NORTH AMERICAN READERS: Please note that conversion charts for cup and spoon measurements and oven temperatures are on page 126.

CONTENTS

CHINA

Chinese is one of the most-travelled and adapted Asian cuisines; from the comparative restraint of Canton cooking to the more zesty offerings of the Szechuan region, it provides adventuresome eating for all tastes. Steamed and braised Chinese food is increasingly popular when the emphasis is on diet and health. When entertaining, Chinese menus for small dinner parties can be stretched to delight larger gatherings. We include cakes and sweets for all occasions.

CHINESE DINNER PARTY FOR EIGHT CANTON-STYLE

- COMBINATION SHORT SOUP
- CRISPY SKIN LEMON CHICKEN
- HONEYED SNOW PEAS AND ASPARAGUS
- RAINBOW BEEF
- FRIED RICE
- BARBECUED PORK SPARE RIBS
- CRUNCHY TOFFEE APPLES

Cantonese food is the most popular type of Chinese food in the world. The food available in the region is varied and versatile, as a result, the combinations seem endless. The food is mostly stir-fried and delicately flavored, relying on the fresh flavors of the food rather than the seasonings.

COMBINATION SHORT SOUP

Make stock the day before serving. Make Wontons several hours before cooking; store in refrigerator, covered with a damp cloth. Add soy sauce according to taste to individual servings.

¼ teaspoon sesame oil
1 chicken breast fillet, chopped
½ bunch Chinese broccoli
250g green prawns, shelled
125g barbecued pork
CHICKEN STOCK
1 boiling chicken
2 carrots, chopped
2 sticks celery, chopped
1 teaspoon whole black peppercorns
3 bay leaves

WONTONS
18 wonton wrappers
125g lean pork mince
1 cup finely chopped cabbage
2 teaspoons light soy sauce
¼ teaspoon sesame oil
½ teaspoon grated fresh ginger
1 egg, beaten

Cut broccoli into 5cm lengths. Heat Chicken Stock in pan, add sesame oil, chicken, broccoli, simmer 2 minutes. Add prawns, pork, simmer few minutes, add Wontons, heat 1 minute.
Chicken Stock: Combine all ingredients in pan, cover with water, bring to boil, reduce heat, simmer, covered, 2 hours; strain. Make stock up to 2 litres with water, cool, refrigerate overnight, lift off fat.

STEP 1:
Wontons: Combine mince, cabbage, soy sauce, sesame oil and ginger. Top each wrapper with teaspoon of filling, brush with egg. Fold diagonally in half.

STEP 2:
Join two corners with egg. Drop Wontons into boiling water, boil, uncovered, until Wontons float, reduce heat, simmer 15 minutes; drain.

CRISPY SKIN LEMON CHICKEN

Serve with boiled rice and chilli and soy sauce for dipping.

8 chicken half breasts (on the bone)
⅓ cup lemon juice
2 tablespoons sugar
1 tablespoon dry sherry
1 teaspoon light soy sauce
cornflour
oil for deep frying
2 teaspoons cornflour, extra
¼ cup chicken stock

Chop each chicken piece into three pieces. Combine lemon juice, sugar, sherry and soy sauce, pour over chicken pieces, marinate 30 minutes. Drain chicken (reserve marinade). Sprinkle chicken all over with cornflour, shake off excess cornflour. Heat oil in wok, add chicken, fry until golden brown and tender; drain on absorbent paper. Remove oil from wok. Pour reserved marinade into clean wok, stir in blended extra cornflour and stock. Stir until mixture boils and thickens, serve over chicken.

HONEYED SNOW PEAS AND ASPARAGUS

250g snow peas
2 bunches asparagus
1 teaspoon sesame oil
1 teaspoon sesame seeds
2 teaspoons honey
¼ teaspoon grated fresh ginger

Top and tail snow peas, peel ends of asparagus with a vegetable peeler; slice asparagus diagonally.

Boil, steam or microwave asparagus until just tender; drain and refresh in cold water. Drop snow peas into pan of boiling water; drain immediately, refresh in cold water. Heat sesame oil and sesame seeds in wok, add snow peas, asparagus, honey and ginger; stir-fry until heated through.

OPPOSITE PAGE:
Combination Short Soup.
ABOVE: Back: Crispy Skin Lemon Chicken; front: Honeyed Snow Peas and Asparagus.

Cane blind and china from Burlington Centre, Sydney.

RAINBOW BEEF

500g beef eye fillet (in one piece)
1 teaspoon teriyaki sauce
1 clove garlic, crushed
1 teaspoon grated fresh ginger
2 teaspoons cornflour
2 teaspoons cornflour, extra
½ cup dry sherry
1 tablespoon light soy sauce
1 tablespoon oyster sauce
¼ cup water
1 tablespoon lemon juice
1 tablespoon sugar
2 tablespoons oil
1 onion, sliced
1 carrot, sliced
1 green pepper, sliced
1 red pepper, sliced

Slice beef finely, cut into thin strips, combine in bowl with teriyaki sauce, garlic, ginger and cornflour, stand 30 minutes. Blend extra cornflour with sherry, soy sauce, oyster sauce, water, lemon juice and sugar. Heat 1 tablespoon of the oil in wok, add beef in batches, stir-fry over high heat; drain. Heat remaining oil in wok. Add onion and carrot, stir-fry few minutes or until just soft, add peppers, stir-fry 2 minutes, add beef.

Add sherry mixture to wok, stir until sauce boils and thickens.

FRIED RICE

4 dried mushrooms
2 cups rice
1 tablespoon oil
1 teaspoon sesame oil
1 clove garlic, crushed
½ teaspoon grated fresh ginger
2 green shallots, chopped
1 small red pepper, chopped
½ x 425g can baby corn, sliced
¼ cucumber, seeded, chopped
100g peas, shelled
1 teaspoon light soy sauce

Cover mushrooms with boiling water, cover, stand 20 minutes; drain. Discard stems and chop mushrooms. Boil rice 12 minutes; drain. Boil peas until just tender; drain.

Heat oil and sesame oil in wok, add garlic, ginger, shallots and pepper, stir-fry 1 minute. Add mushrooms, corn, cucumber and peas, stir-fry 2 minutes, add soy sauce. Add rice, stir-fry until heated right through.

BARBECUED PORK SPARE RIBS

These spare ribs are obtainable from some butchers. Ask for American-style pork ribs.

1kg pork spare ribs
1 tablespoon honey
1 tablespoon oil
¼ teaspoon five spice powder
1 tablespoon hoisin sauce
2 tablespoons light soy sauce
¼ cup dry sherry
2 cloves garlic, crushed

Place ribs in baking dish. Combine remaining ingredients, pour over pork, bake in moderately hot oven 20 minutes, reduce to moderate. Bake further 20 minutes or until tender, basting several times during cooking.

BELOW: From left: Rainbow Beef, Fried Rice, Barbecued Pork Spare Ribs.
OPPOSITE PAGE: Crunchy Toffee Apples.

CRUNCHY TOFFEE APPLES

Apples can be battered and fried several hours in advance and coated with the toffee at the table.

4 Granny Smith apples, peeled
oil for deep frying
BATTER
2 cups self-raising flour
1 tablespoon oil
2 cups water
TOFFEE
1 tablespoon oil
1 cup water
2 cups sugar
1 tablespoon sesame seeds

Cut apples into eight pieces, remove cores from apples.

Batter: Sift flour into bowl, make well in centre, stir in oil and water, stir until smooth. Drop apple into Batter; drain off excess Batter, deep fry in hot oil until golden brown; drain apple pieces on absorbent paper.

Toffee: Heat oil in pan, add water and sugar, stir without boiling until sugar is dissolved. Increase heat to high, boil 5 to 10 minutes without stirring, until Toffee turns light golden color. Remove from heat, add sesame seeds. Dip 1 piece of apple into toffee at a time. Remove immediately with oiled tongs and place in a bowl of iced water. Repeat with remaining pieces of apple. See picture, at right.

CHINESE DINNER PARTY FOR SIX PEKING-STYLE

MONGOLIAN LAMB

CHILLI KING PRAWNS

FRIED NOODLES WITH VEGETABLES

DOUBLE-FRIED SHREDDED BEEF

PEKING DUCK

PINK SUGAR PUFFS

The food from the Peking region is usually plain but robust in flavor. Noodles are often served in place of rice, and much of the food is deep fried, sometimes coated in a light batter. The region is famous for Peking Duck and ducks bred solely for this dish are roasted in a special oven. We've included a simplified version of this delicacy for a sumptuous, memorable dinner party.

MONGOLIAN LAMB
1½kg boned leg of lamb
2 teaspoons sugar
2 tablespoons light soy sauce
1 teaspoon bean sauce
2 cloves garlic, crushed
1 egg
1 tablespoon oil
1 tablespoon cornflour
¼ cup oil, extra
4 medium onions, quartered
½ cup chicken stock
2 teaspoons bean sauce, extra
1 teaspoon cornflour, extra
3 green shallots, chopped

Trim lamb of sinew and fat; slice lamb thinly. Combine sugar, soy sauce, bean sauce, garlic, egg, oil and cornflour. Add lamb, cover, marinate 30 minutes. Heat extra oil in wok, add onions, stir-fry until soft; remove from wok. Add lamb mixture in several batches, stir-fry each batch until lamb is well browned, continue with remaining lamb. Return lamb to wok, stir in blended stock, extra bean sauce and extra cornflour, stir-fry until mixture boils and thickens. Add reserved onion and shallots, heat before serving.

LEFT: Back: Mongolian Lamb; front: Chilli King Prawns.
OPPOSITE PAGE: From left: Fried Noodles with Vegetables, Double-Fried Shredded Beef.

Chest of drawers from Eastern Emporium, Sydney; background screen from China Art and Furniture Co. (Imports), Sydney.

CHILLI KING PRAWNS

1kg green king prawns, shelled
1 cup plain flour
⅓ cup cornflour
1 egg white
1¼ cups water
oil for deep frying
1 tablespoon oil, extra
1 tablespoon grated fresh ginger
3 cloves garlic, crushed
2 tablespoons tomato sauce
1 tablespoon chilli sauce
2 teaspoons sugar
1 tablespoon light soy sauce
1 tablespoon dry sherry
¼ cup water

Devein prawns. Cut prawns in half lengthways, although not all the way through; flatten prawns gently with blade of large knife or cleaver.

Sift flour and cornflour into bowl, make a well in centre, gradually stir in combined egg white and water. Mix to a smooth batter. Heat oil in wok, dip prawns in batter; drain excess batter before deep frying in hot oil until prawns are pale golden brown; drain on absorbent paper.

Heat extra oil in wok, add ginger, garlic, tomato sauce, chilli sauce, sugar, soy sauce, sherry and water. Bring to boil, reduce heat, simmer 2 minutes, add prawns, reheat, before serving.

FRIED NOODLES WITH VEGETABLES

250g packet thin fresh or frozen egg
    noodles
oil for deep frying
1 tablespoon oil, extra
1 carrot, sliced
1 cup small broccoli flowerets
1 cup bean sprouts
100g snow peas
1½ tablespoons cornflour
2 tablespoons crunchy peanut butter
1 teaspoon oyster sauce
2 teaspoons light soy sauce
2 tablespoons dry sherry
3 cups chicken stock

Fry noodles in deep hot oil for 2 seconds or until puffed (see picture, below) remove immediately; drain on absorbent paper.

Heat extra oil in wok. Add carrot; stir-fry, add broccoli; stir-fry, add bean sprouts and snow peas; stir-fry. Blend cornflour with peanut butter, oyster sauce, soy sauce, sherry and stock, add to pan with vegetables. Stir until mixture boils and thickens, stir in half the noodles. Place remaining noodles on serving plate, top with vegetable mixture. Serve immediately.

DOUBLE-FRIED SHREDDED BEEF

500g beef eye fillet
2 teaspoons oil
2 tablespoons water
1 teaspoon cornflour
1 large carrot
2 tablespoons cornflour, extra
oil for deep frying
SAUCE
1 tablespoon oil
1 green shallot, sliced
1 clove garlic, sliced
¼ teaspoon chopped fresh chilli
3 teaspoons white vinegar
2 teaspoons dry sherry
2 teaspoons dark soy sauce
1 tablespoon water
2 teaspoons sugar
½ teaspoon sesame oil

Remove fat and sinew from beef; slice beef thinly, then cut into fine shreds. Combine beef with oil, water and cornflour. Cover, marinate 30 minutes.

Slice carrot thinly, cut into fine strips. Heat oil for deep frying in wok, add carrot, cook until lightly browned, remove from wok, reserve. Reheat oil, add meat, cook a few minutes or until tender, stirring gently to separate meat; drain. Heat oil again. Sprinkle extra cornflour evenly over beef. Deep fry beef again in hot oil until golden brown; drain. Add to Sauce with reserved carrot, reheat thoroughly before serving immediately.

Sauce: Heat oil in wok, add shallot, garlic, chilli. Add remaining ingredients, bring to boil, stir in beef and carrot.

PEKING DUCK

Bake duck as close to serving time as possible. Make Pancakes up to one day in advance, reheat in steamer or microwave oven.

No 15 duck
2 tablespoons honey
2 tablespoons dry sherry
1 tablespoon brown vinegar
1 cucumber, peeled
6 green shallots
DIPPING SAUCE
1 tablespoon bean sauce
2 tablespoons plum sauce
1 tablespoon light soy sauce
¼ teaspoon sesame oil
PANCAKES
2 cups plain flour
1 cup boiling water
1 teaspoon sesame oil

Lower duck into pan of boiling water, cover, bring to boil, remove from heat; stand 30 minutes. Drain duck, pat dry with absorbent paper; stand at room temperature, uncovered, until cold. Brush duck evenly with combined honey, sherry and vinegar, place on rack over baking dish, refrigerate 15 minutes uncovered. Baste duck again with honey mixture, refrigerate uncovered overnight. Bake in moderate oven 40 minutes or until duck is golden brown, crisp and tender. Cut cucumber in half lengthways, scoop out seeds, cut cucumber into thin strips; cut shallots into thin strips. Carve duck into thin slices.
Dipping Sauce: Combine all ingredients; mix well.

STEP 1

Pancakes: Sift flour into bowl, make well in centre, add boiling water and sesame oil all at once, mix to a soft sticky dough. Knead about 10 minutes on lightly floured surface until smooth. Cover, rest 15 minutes. Roll into a sausage shape, cut dough into about 35 pieces.

STEP 2
Roll each piece into a 10cm circle.

STEP 3
Heat a pan, dry fry pancakes on both sides for about 20 seconds.

To serve: Spread hot Pancakes with Dipping Sauce, top with cucumber, shallot and duck, roll, eat with fingers.

PINK SUGAR PUFFS
1 cup water
30g butter
1 cup plain flour
5 eggs
oil for deep frying
⅓ cup castor sugar
few drops pink food coloring

Place water and butter in pan, bring to boil, stir until butter is melted. Add sifted flour all at once, stir until mixture forms a ball and leaves sides of pan, remove from heat; cool 5 minutes. Beat mixture in small bowl with electric mixer for about 10 seconds or until smooth, add eggs, one at a time, beating well after each addition. Beat about 5 minutes or until mixture is smooth and glossy. Heat oil in wok, drop teaspoonfuls of mixture into hot oil. Cook until Puffs stop rising and brown lightly; drain on absorbent paper. Toss in Pink Sugar, serve immediately.
Pink Sugar: Place sugar in plastic bag, add a drop or two of pink food coloring, hold bag closed with one hand and work coloring evenly through sugar with other hand.

LEFT: Peking Duck
RIGHT: Pink Sugar Puffs

Bamboo plant from The Flower Man, Double Bay, NSW.

CHINESE
LIGHT AND EASY DINNER PARTY FOR SIX

STIR-FRIED BEAN SPROUTS AND MUSHROOMS

PRAWN-STUFFED SQUID

PORK IN FRESH PLUM SAUCE

MARINATED SHALLOT CHICKEN

CREAMED CHINESE CABBAGE

GOLDEN STEAMED CAKE

The food in this menu features different flavors, textures and cooking methods. Serve the dishes in any order you choose. Organise the cooking so the Golden Steamed Cake can be served the minute it comes out of the steamer.

STIR-FRIED BEAN SPROUTS AND MUSHROOMS
250g bean sprouts
10 dried mushrooms
4 green shallots
2 tablespoons oil
1 clove garlic, crushed
1 tablespoon oyster sauce
2 teaspoons light soy sauce
2 teaspoons dry sherry
2 teaspoons cornflour
¼ cup water
Soak mushrooms in boiling water 20 minutes; drain. Remove and discard stems, chop caps finely. Wash and drain bean sprouts, slice shallots diagonally. Heat oil in wok, add garlic, mushrooms and shallots, stir-fry 1 minute. Add bean sprouts, toss through, add sauces, sherry and blended cornflour and water. Stir-fry until mixture boils and thickens.

Back: Stir-Fried Bean Sprouts and Mushrooms; front: Prawn-Stuffed Squid.

China is Black Renaissance by Fitz and Floyd.

PRAWN-STUFFED SQUID

Squid can be assembled, covered and refrigerated up to one day ahead. Cook just before serving. You will need ¼ cup uncooked rice for this recipe.

4 small squid hoods
6 dried mushrooms
½ small red pepper, finely chopped
375g green prawns, shelled
2 green shallots, chopped
½ teaspoon sesame oil
2 teaspoons light soy sauce
1 clove garlic, crushed
½ x 140g can water chestnuts, chopped
¾ cup cooked rice
⅓ cup hoisin sauce
1 tablespoon light soy sauce, extra
Remove any membrane from outside of squid. Cover mushrooms in boiling water, stand 20 minutes; drain, remove and discard stems.

STEP 1
Mince or very finely chop prawns, combine with chopped mushroom caps, red pepper, shallots, sesame oil, soy sauce, garlic, water chestnuts and rice. Spoon mixture into squid hoods.

STEP 2
Using a needle and cotton, sew tops of squid together. Place in single layer in bamboo steamer over wok or pan of boiling water. Cover, cook 15 minutes or until tender. Cut sewn ends off; discard. Slice squid, serve with combined hoisin and extra soy sauce.

12

GLAZED HONEY QUAIL

6 quail
2½ tablespoons dark soy sauce
2 teaspoons dry sherry
¼ teaspoon five spice powder
½ teaspoon grated fresh ginger
2 tablespoons honey
oil

Cut quail in half by cutting through breast lengthwise. Drop quail into pan of boiling water, boil 1 minute; drain. Add quail to combined soy sauce, sherry, five spice powder and ginger; mix well, cover, marinate 1 hour, turning occasionally.

Remove quail from marinade, brush thoroughly with honey twice. Place quail over wire rack, dry for 30 minutes. Barbecue quail over low heat, turning frequently and basting with oil, for about 15 minutes. Or, bake on rack over baking dish in moderate oven for about 30 minutes.

PINEAPPLE FRIED RICE

Rice mixture can be prepared the day before and reheated in the pineapple shells on day of serving.

1 large pineapple
2 cups rice
4 green shallots, chopped
1 teaspoon curry powder
1 red pepper, chopped
140g can water chestnuts, drained, chopped
2 teaspoons dark soy sauce
¼ cup toasted almonds

Cut pineapple in half lengthwise. Cut out flesh of pineapple without breaking skin, dice flesh finely. Cook rice in boiling water 12 minutes; drain.

Combine rice, shallots, curry powder, pepper, water chestnuts and soy sauce with pineapple in bowl. Spoon rice into pineapple shells, wrap completely in heavy foil, barbecue over low heat for about 20 minutes or until heated through (or bake in moderate oven 10 minutes). Sprinkle with almonds before serving.

LYCHEE ICECREAM WITH MANDARIN SAUCE

Mandarin liqueur gives a delicious flavor to this recipe. If difficult to obtain substitute brandy.

3 eggs
½ cup castor sugar
2 x 300ml cartons thickened cream
2 x 565g cans lychees, drained
MANDARIN SAUCE
2 x 310g cans mandarin oranges
2 tablespoons mandarin liqueur
1 tablespoon cornflour
1 tablespoon water

Place eggs and sugar in pan, whisk over low heat without boiling until frothy, remove from heat, place in large bowl, cool to room temperature. Beat cream until firm peaks form, fold into egg mixture. Puree lychees in blender or processor, fold into cream mixture. Pour into deep cake tin, cover, freeze several hours until partly frozen. Place into large basin, beat with electric mixer until smooth. Pour into deep cake tin, cover, freeze several hours or overnight until set. Serve with Mandarin Sauce and extra mandarin oranges and lychees if desired.

Mandarin Sauce: Drain mandarins, reserve ½ cup syrup. Puree mandarins in blender or processor, pour into pan. Stir in reserved syrup, liqueur and blended cornflour and water. Stir over heat until Sauce boils and thickens.

Lychee Icecream with Mandarin Sauce.

Glass dishes by Orrefors.

CHINESE HOT AND SPICY DINNER PARTY FOR SIX

- SCALLOPS WITH CORIANDER
- PORK AND VEGETABLE MEDLEY
- CHICKEN WITH CRISPY RICE
- CHILLI PLUM BEEF
- DEEP FRIED FISH WITH RED GARLIC SAUCE
- MALTED ALMOND ICECREAM

The recipes we have chosen for this menu are hot and full of flavor. We have kept the chilli content quite low in our recipes but you can adjust the heat of each dish by increasing the fresh or dried chilli. The delicious Malted Almond Icecream is a refreshing end to this superb dinner party. Serve the various courses in the order suggested above.

SCALLOPS WITH CORIANDER
250g scallops
1 green shallot
3cm piece fresh ginger
1 cup chicken stock
1 teaspoon cornflour
2 teaspoons chopped fresh coriander
¼ teaspoon chopped fresh red chilli
1 clove garlic, crushed
¼ teaspoon sugar

Devein scallops. Cut shallot and ginger into thin strips. Heat half the stock in pan, add scallops, simmer 1 minute or until scallops are just cooked; drain. Blend cornflour with remaining stock in pan, add shallot, ginger, coriander, chilli, garlic and sugar, stir until sauce boils and thickens. Divide scallops between 6 scallop shells or small serving dishes, top scallops with hot sauce, serve immediately.

ABOVE: From left: Deep Fried Fish with Red Garlic Sauce, Scallops with Coriander.

19

DEEP FRIED FISH WITH RED GARLIC SAUCE

We used red fish fillets for this recipe.

500g small fish fillets
⅔ cup plain flour
⅓ cup cornflour
2 egg whites
1 tablespoon oil
1 cup water
oil for deep frying
RED GARLIC SAUCE
¼ cup sugar
1 teaspoon salt
1 tablespoon white vinegar
½ teaspoon chilli powder
2 tablespoons dry sherry
2 cloves garlic, crushed
1 tablespoon cornflour
1 cup water
2 drops red food coloring

Remove bones from fish; cut fish in half. Sift flour and cornflour into bowl, make well in centre, stir in egg whites and oil, then gradually stir in water to give a thin smooth paste.

Heat oil for deep frying in wok, dip fish in batter; drain well. Deep fry in hot oil until golden brown and tender; drain. Heat Red Garlic Sauce in wok, add fish, cook until hot.

Red Garlic Sauce: Combine sugar, salt, vinegar, chilli powder, sherry and garlic in pan, stir in blended cornflour, water and coloring, stir until Sauce boils and thickens; strain before using.

PORK AND VEGETABLE MEDLEY

6 dried mushrooms
1 tablespoon oil
125g barbecued pork, chopped
1 tablespoon oil, extra
1 tablespoon bean sauce
1 tablespoon dark soy sauce
½ teaspoon chilli sauce
2 teaspoons sugar
1 teaspoon grated fresh ginger
2 sticks celery, chopped
2 carrots, chopped
1 green pepper, chopped
1 red pepper, chopped
425g can baby corn, drained
¼ cup chicken stock
2 green shallots, finely chopped

Cover mushrooms with boiling water, stand 20 minutes; drain. Remove and discard stems, chop caps finely. Heat oil in wok, add pork, stir-fry 1 minute, remove from wok. Heat extra oil in wok, add sauces, sugar and ginger, stir-fry 30 seconds. Add mushrooms, celery, carrots, peppers and corn, stir-fry few minutes, add pork, stock and shallots, stir-fry until heated through.

CHICKEN WITH CRISPY RICE

Make rice the day before required.

2 cups short grain rice
2 small pieces canned bamboo shoot
1 tablespoon oil
1 onion, chopped
1 red pepper, chopped
2 chicken breast fillets, chopped
60g barbecued pork, chopped
2 green shallots, chopped
3 tablespoons tomato sauce
2 teaspoons sugar
3 teaspoons vinegar
1 teaspoon grated fresh ginger
3 teaspoons dark soy sauce
2 teaspoons cornflour
1 cup water
oil for deep frying

Place rice in small pan, pour in enough water to cover top of rice by 3cm.

Cover with tight-fitting lid, heat until simmering, reduce heat, cook 30 minutes, or until water is absorbed and rice is tender. Remove lid, leave rice in pan, stand overnight to dry out.

Turn rice onto board, cut into thick squares. Deep fry in hot oil until crisp as shown at right. Cut bamboo shoot into fine strips. Heat oil in wok, add onion, stir-fry few minutes, add pepper and chicken, stir-fry few minutes, add pork, shallots and bamboo shoots, stir-fry 1 minute; remove from wok. Add combined tomato sauce, sugar, vinegar, ginger, soy sauce, and blended cornflour and water to wok. Stir until mixture boils and thickens. Return chicken and vegetable mixture to wok, stir-fry 1 minute to heat before pouring over rice squares.

CHILLI PLUM BEEF

750g beef eye fillet (in one piece)
150ml bottle plum sauce
1 tablespoon dark soy sauce
1 clove garlic, crushed
1 teaspoon grated fresh ginger
½ teaspoon chopped fresh red chilli
2 teaspoons sugar
2 teaspoons dry sherry
2 teaspoons cornflour
2 tablespoons oil
½ cup water
2 teaspoons cornflour, extra
1 beef stock cube

Trim beef, slice thinly. Combine beef, sauces, garlic, ginger, chilli, sugar, sherry and cornflour in large bowl, mix well, cover, marinate 30 minutes or refrigerate overnight. Heat a little of the oil in a wok, add beef, about a quarter at a time, stir-fry few minutes, or until browned. Remove from wok as it is cooked; repeat with remaining oil and beef. Return beef to wok with remaining marinade, blended water and extra cornflour and crumbled stock cube, stir until mixture boils and thickens.

MALTED ALMOND ICECREAM

Icecream can be made several days in advance; keep covered with foil in freezer until needed.

2 x 300ml cartons thickened cream
½ cup maltose
⅓ cup brown sugar
6 eggs, separated
2 tablespoons flaked almonds

Heat cream, maltose and brown sugar in a pan until mixture comes to the boil. Remove from heat, cool 5 minutes, whisk in egg yolks. Beat egg whites in medium bowl with electric mixer until firm peaks form, fold into egg yolk mixture. Pour into large loaf tin, cover with foil, freeze several hours or until set. Beat mixture in large bowl with electric mixer until smooth, return to tin, cover, freeze several hours or overnight until set. Toast almonds on oven tray in moderate oven for 5 minutes; cool. Serve Icecream topped with cream, a little honey and the almonds.

LEFT: Back, from left: Pork and Vegetable Medley, Chicken with Crispy Rice; front: Chilli Plum Beef.
ABOVE: Malted Almond Icecream.

CHINESE
YUM CHA
FOR EIGHT

CRUNCHY PORK CASES

BACON AND FISH ROLLS

CHINESE RICE BALLS

SHALLOT AND SESAME PUFFS

CRISPY PRAWN AND SCALLOP BALLS

CHICKEN AND PORK BUNS

DATE AND LYCHEE WONTONS

CUSTARD TARTS

Traditionally, Yum Cha is served between 10am and 3pm, one dish at a time. The order doesn't really matter so sweets do not necessarily come last. The order suggested is the easiest to follow for cooking purposes. Choose a fragrant Chinese tea for your guests and serve it throughout Yum Cha. Serve soy and chilli sauce for dipping when serving the savory foods.

BACON AND FISH ROLLS

Rolls can be prepared, covered and refrigerated up to a day before battering and frying them. We used ling fish fillets in this recipe.

375g white fish fillets
100g baby mushrooms
3 green shallots
6 large bacon rashers
oil for deep frying
BATTER
½ cup cornflour
½ cup plain flour
¾ cup water
1 egg, separated

Cut fish into chunks. Remove stalks from mushrooms, cut caps in half, cut shallots into 6cm lengths. Remove rind and most of the fat from bacon, cut each rasher into three pieces.

STEP 1

Place one piece of fish, mushroom and shallot on one end of each piece of bacon; roll up tightly, firmly secure roll with toothpick.

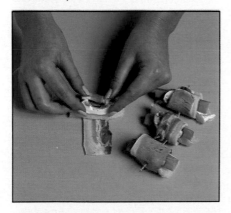

STEP 2

Dip rolls into Batter, deep fry in hot oil until golden brown; drain.
Batter: Sift cornflour and flour into bowl, gradually stir in water and egg yolk, stir until smooth (or blend or process until smooth). Beat egg white in small bowl until soft peaks form, lightly fold into batter.
Makes 18.

CRUNCHY PORK CASES

Spring Roll Cases can be fried up to a day before required, cooled, wrapped tightly and stored in a dry place. Reheat in moderate oven about 10 minutes before filling and serving. Pork filling can be made up to two days ahead, refrigerated and reheated when ready to serve (add shallots and sprouts after reheating).

500g pork mince
6 dried mushrooms
1 tablespoon oil
2 teaspoons cornflour
2 teaspoons light soy sauce
2 teaspoons oyster sauce
6 green shallots, chopped
1 cup (100g) bean sprouts
SPRING ROLL CASES
4 spring roll wrappers (21cm square)
oil for deep frying

Cover mushrooms with boiling water, stand 20 minutes; drain, reserve ⅓ cup liquid. Remove and discard stems of mushrooms, chop caps finely.

Heat oil in wok, add pork, stir-fry until crisp and well browned; drain excess oil. Blend cornflour with reserved liquid and sauces, add to pork, stir constantly over heat until mixture boils and thickens. Stir in shallots and sprouts, spoon mixture into hot Spring Roll Cases.

STEP 1

Spring Roll Cases: Cut each wrapper into 9 squares. Take 2 squares, place one on top of the other as shown.

STEP 2

Heat oil in wok, gently lower wrapper into oil, immediately press base of small soup ladle or spoon into centre of wrapper. Hold in this position for about 5 seconds or until wrapper is set. Remove ladle or spoon, fry further 5 seconds or until golden brown; drain.
Makes 18.

CHINESE RICE BALLS

Balls can be prepared up to a day before required. Keep covered in refrigerator. Roll balls in rice just before steaming and serving.

1 cup rice
300g minced pork
8 dried mushrooms
300g can bamboo shoots, drained
1 tablespoon light soy sauce
1 tablespoon dry sherry
1 teaspoon grated fresh ginger
2 green shallots, finely chopped
1 clove garlic, crushed
2 egg whites
DIPPING SAUCE
2 tablespoons light soy sauce
1 tablespoon grated fresh ginger

Cover rice with cold water, stand 2 hours; drain well. Cover mushrooms with boiling water, stand 20 minutes. Drain mushrooms, remove and discard stems, chop mushroom caps finely, chop bamboo shoots finely. Combine pork, mushrooms, bamboo shoots, soy sauce, sherry, ginger, shallots, garlic and egg whites; mix well. Shape teaspoonfuls of mixture into balls, roll balls over rice (see picture below) until well coated. Place balls in steamer so that they are not touching, cover, steam over simmering water 15 minutes. Cool in steamer 2 minutes before serving with Dipping Sauce.
Dipping Sauce: Combine soy sauce and ginger.
Makes about 20.

Clockwise from front: Shallot and Sesame Puffs, Crunchy Pork Cases, Chicken and Pork Buns, Chinese Rice Balls, Crispy Prawn and Scallop Balls, Bacon and Fish Rolls.

Bamboo table from Eastern Emporium, Sydney.

23

CHICKEN AND PORK BUNS

2 chicken breast fillets
100g barbecued pork
4 dried mushrooms
230g can water chestnuts, drained
2 teaspoons cornflour
1 teaspoon dry sherry
3 green shallots, finely chopped
1 teaspoon grated fresh ginger
2 tablespoons oil
SAUCE
1 tablespoon dry sherry
1 tablespoon soy sauce
1 teaspoon sesame oil
½ teaspoon sugar
¼ cup water
PASTRY
2 cups plain flour
3 teaspoons baking powder
1 tablespoon sugar
1 tablespoon oil
¾ cup warm water

Cover mushrooms with boiling water, stand 20 minutes. Drain mushrooms, remove and discard stems, chop caps finely. Chop water chestnuts finely.

Chop chicken and pork finely, combine with cornflour and sherry. Heat oil in wok, add shallots and ginger, stir-fry 1 minute. Add chicken and pork, water chestnuts and mushrooms, stir-fry until chicken is just tender. Add Sauce, stir until mixture boils. Remove from heat, cool to room temperature.
Sauce: Combine all ingredients.

STEP 1

Pastry: Sift flour, baking powder and sugar into bowl, make well in centre, gradually stir in oil and water, mix to a soft pliable dough. Turn onto lightly floured surface, knead lightly until smooth. Cover dough with plastic food wrap, stand 10 minutes. Divide dough in half, roll each half into a sausage shape, cut each sausage into 8 equal pieces. Flatten each piece with palm of hand, roll out to 9 cm rounds.

STEP 2

Place a tablespoon of filling in centre of each round, gather edges together, twist firmly.

Place buns on greaseproof paper in steamer, do not have buns touching, cover, steam over simmering water about 10 minutes, or until firm.
Makes 16.

CRISPY PRAWN AND SCALLOP BALLS

Prepare balls to frying stage up to a day ahead if desired. Dust in cornflour before frying. Balls can also be steamed instead of fried — they will take about 10 minutes.

16 (about 250g) scallops
375g green prawns
125g ham
3 green shallots, chopped
2 tablespoons finely chopped
   blanched almonds
¼ cup finely chopped Chinese mixed
   pickles
2 teaspoons light soy sauce
1 tablespoon cornflour
¼ cup cornflour, extra
oil for deep frying

Devein scallops, remove and reserve coral. Poach scallops in pan with enough water to just cover them, simmer a minute or two, or until scallops are just tender; drain. Shell and devein prawns. Mince or finely chop prawns, ham and coral, stir in shallots, almonds, pickles, soy sauce and cornflour. Mould mixture around scallops, dust lightly with extra cornflour (see picture below). Deep fry in hot oil until golden brown; drain.
Makes about 16.

SHALLOT AND SESAME PUFFS

2 sheets ready rolled shortcrust
   pastry
1 tablespoon oil
1 teaspoon grated fresh ginger
1 clove garlic, crushed
12 green shallots, sliced
½ cup sesame seeds
2 tablespoons oyster sauce
1 egg yolk
sesame seeds, extra
oil for deep frying

Heat oil in wok, add ginger, garlic, shallots and sesame seeds, stir-fry 1 minute, add oyster sauce; cool.

Cut eight 8cm squares from pastry sheets, place a tablespoon of shallot mixture onto each square, glaze edges with egg, bring the four corners to the centre (see picture below), pinch edges together gently. Glaze with remaining egg yolk, sprinkle lightly with extra sesame seeds. Deep fry in hot oil until golden brown.
Makes 16.

DATE AND LYCHEE WONTONS

Wontons can be prepared up to several hours before frying. Keep covered with damp cloth in refrigerator.

24 wonton wrappers (7cm square)
200g fresh dates
425g can lychees
½ cup finely chopped walnuts
1 tablespoon grated lemon rind
2 tablespoons lemon juice
oil for deep frying

Remove skin and seeds from dates, chop dates finely. Press lychees gently between sheets of absorbent paper, chop lychees finely. Combine dates, lychees, walnuts, lemon rind and juice.

Place a teaspoon of mixture in centre of each wrapper, gather sides around filling, pinch edges together (see picture below). Heat oil in wok, deep fry Wontons until golden brown. Drain on absorbent paper, dust with icing sugar before serving.

Makes 24.

OPPOSITE PAGE: In descending order: Chicken and Pork Buns, Shallot and Sesame Puffs, Crispy Prawn and Scallop Balls. BELOW: From top: Date and Lychee Wontons, Custard Tarts.

Tiered platter from Dansab Pty. Ltd., Sydney; screen from Burlington Centre, Sydney; tree from The Flower Man, Double Bay, NSW.

CUSTARD TARTS (DARN TARTS)

These tarts are best eaten warm on day of making, but they can be made the day before required and kept covered and refrigerated. Lard and butter must be refrigerator-cold.

WATER DOUGH
¾ cup plain flour
⅓ cup water
FAT DOUGH
½ cup plain flour
125g lard
125g butter
CUSTARD
¾ cup sugar
1¼ cups water
5 eggs
½ cup milk

Water Dough: Sift flour into bowl, stir in enough water to mix to a firm dough. Knead on lightly floured surface until smooth, roll out to rectangle 8cm x 12cm. Wrap rectangle carefully in plastic food wrap, refrigerate 30 minutes.
Fat Dough: Sift flour into bowl, rub in lard and butter, wrap in plastic food wrap, refrigerate 30 minutes, or until firm. Roll dough on floured surface to a rectangle 12cm x 15cm.
Custard: Combine sugar and water in pan, stir over heat without boiling until sugar is dissolved; cool. Combine sugar syrup, eggs and milk in bowl, beat with fork until combined.

STEP 1

To Make Tarts: Place Water Dough rectangle on one end of Fat Dough rectangle. Fold other end of Fat Dough over to cover Water Dough.

Turn dough around so that the fold is on your left hand side, roll to a rectangle 12cm x 30cm.

STEP 2

Fold short ends in to meet in the centre, fold in half again at the centre. Repeat rolling and folding, 3 more times making sure the fold is always on your left hand side.

STEP 3

Roll dough out thinly to about 2mm, cut into 9cm circles with a sharp fluted cutter, press into deep fluted tart tins (¼ cup capacity). Pour Custard carefully into pastry cases, bake in hot oven 10 minutes, reduce heat to moderately hot, cook further 15 minutes or until custard is set.

Makes about 20.

CHINESE
SUMMERTIME DINNER PARTY FOR FOUR

EGG ROLLS WITH
CORIANDER SAUCE

ROAST DUCK WITH FRUIT
SAUCE

GINGER BROCCOLI

SEAFOOD AND
VEGETABLES ON LETTUCE

CHILLED MELON AND
SAGO DESSERT

This is an ideal menu for a lunch or light evening meal when the weather is warm. Serve the food in the order suggested for easy cooking. Serve the main part of the meal with rice, seasoned salt (see Glossary) and soy sauce with a little chopped fresh ginger for dipping. The fresh tasting chilled dessert is a perfect finish to this summertime dinner gathering.

ROAST DUCK WITH FRUIT SAUCE

Serve with a dipping sauce made with a tablespoon chilli sauce, mixed with a teaspoon dark soy sauce.

No 15 duck
1 tablespoon honey
1 tablespoon dark soy sauce
1 tablespoon oil
FRUIT SAUCE
2 oranges
1 cup orange juice
1 tablespoon honey
¼ cup lemon juice
1 teaspoon light soy sauce
1 teaspoon dark soy sauce
½ cup chicken stock
1 tablespoon cornflour
1 tablespoon water
425g can lychees, drained
450g can pineapple pieces, drained

Remove neck from duck. Rinse duck, pat dry inside and out. Tuck wings under body. Brush combined honey and soy sauce over duck. Place duck on rack in baking dish, refrigerate uncovered overnight to dry. Brush duck with oil, bake in moderate oven 1 hour or until tender. Cut duck into pieces, serve with Fruit Sauce.

Fruit Sauce: Cut oranges into segments. Using sharp knife, peel oranges thickly, removing all white pith. Cut down between segments, as close as possible to joining membranes. Segments will come away neatly. Combine orange juice, honey, lemon juice, soy sauces, stock and blended cornflour and water in wok, stir constantly over heat until Sauce boils and thickens. Stir in lychees, pineapple and oranges.

LEFT: Roast Duck with Fruit Sauce.

EGG ROLLS WITH CORIANDER SAUCE

Egg rolls can be prepared up to several hours before steaming.

4 chicken breast fillets
1 tablespoon dry sherry
1 green shallot, chopped
4 eggs
2 tablespoons water
6 spinach leaves
oil
CORIANDER SAUCE
2 cups chicken stock
1 tablespoon chopped coriander
3 teaspoons cornflour
3 teaspoons water

Marinate chicken in sherry for about 30 minutes. Process or mince chicken until smooth; stir in shallot. Beat eggs and water together with fork. Lightly oil wok, heat, pour in enough egg mixture to make an omelet about 12cm in diameter. Turn wok to make omelet as round as possible, cook until just set, remove from wok, repeat with remaining egg mixture. You should have 6 to 8 omelets.

Remove stalks from spinach, drop leaves into pan of boiling water; drain immediately. Spread spinach leaves over omelet, trim spinach to fit omelets; spread with chicken mixture, roll up firmly like a swiss roll. Place rolls in single layer on plate or in bamboo steamer. Place tripod in wok, add enough water to come within 1cm of top of tripod, bring water to boil.

Place plate or steamer on top of tripod, cover wok, steam about 10 minutes. Serve with Coriander Sauce.

Coriander Sauce: Combine stock and coriander in pan, bring to boil, reduce heat, simmer 5 minutes uncovered. Strain stock, discard coriander, return stock to pan, add blended cornflour and water, stir constantly until Sauce boils and thickens.

SEAFOOD AND VEGETABLES ON LETTUCE

250g green king prawns
250g scallops
250g squid
¼ teaspoon sugar
1 teaspoon cornflour
½ x 425g can young corn, drained
3 green shallots
150g can champignons, drained
1 carrot, sliced
½ cup chicken stock
½ cup oil
½ small lettuce, shredded
1 teaspoon sesame oil
2 teaspoons oyster sauce

Shell and devein prawns; clean squid. Cut squid in half, spread out flat with the inside facing up, mark in a diamond pattern with a sharp knife; cut squid into diagonal pieces. Combine prawns, scallops and squid with sugar and cornflour.

Slice corn in half lengthways, cut shallots into 4cm lengths. Combine corn, champignons, carrot and stock in pan, bring to boil, boil 2 minutes. Drain vegetables, reserve stock.

Heat oil in wok, add seafood, stir-fry until just tender; drain oil from wok except for 1 tablespoon, heat. Combine oyster sauce, and sesame oil with 2 tablespoons of reserved stock. Add seafood, prepared vegetables and shallots, stir-fry 1 minute. Add sesame oil mixture, stir-fry until mixture boils and thickens. Turn seafood mixture onto lettuce; serve.

GINGER BROCCOLI

750g broccoli
5cm piece fresh ginger, peeled, sliced
1 green shallot, chopped
1 cup water
1 tablespoon oil
1 tablespoon light soy sauce
2 teaspoons dry sherry
2 teaspoons sugar
2 tablespoons toasted slivered almonds

Cut broccoli into flowerets, place in pan with ginger, shallot and water, bring to boil, boil until tender; drain. Discard ginger and shallot. Heat oil, soy sauce, sherry and sugar in wok, pour over broccoli. Sprinkle broccoli with almonds.

CHILLED MELON AND SAGO DESSERT

Use the melon of your choice in this recipe. Dessert can be made and refrigerated a day before serving. Sago or tapioca can be used in this recipe. We served our dessert in a hollowed-out honeydew melon shell. This dessert does not set; serve it with a spoon.

¼ cup sago
2 cups water
⅓ cup sugar
small piece watermelon
⅓ cup canned coconut cream

Bring water to the boil in pan, add sago, simmer uncovered 10 minutes or until sago is clear. Add sugar, stir until dissolved. Puree watermelon pulp, you will need 1 cup pulp. Stir into sago mixture with coconut cream. Refrigerate covered, until cold.

LEFT: In descending order: Seafood and Vegetables on Lettuce, Ginger Broccoli, Egg Rolls with Coriander Sauce.
BELOW: Chilled Melon and Sago Dessert.

CHINESE COCKTAIL PARTY FOR 15

CRAB-STUFFED MUSHROOMS

OYSTERS WITH BARBECUED PORK

SESAME BEEF BALLS

CHINESE MIXED VEGETABLES

FISH AND HAM PUFFS

STUFFED CHICKEN WINGS

SATE CHICKEN DRUMS

Try serving oriental flavored food at your next cocktail party — the titbits are irresistible and blend so well with cocktails.

CRAB-STUFFED MUSHROOMS

Prepare mushrooms, ready for frying, several hours ahead if desired.

36 (250g) small mushrooms
60g pork mince
1 teaspoon dark soy sauce
1 teaspoon sugar
1 teaspoon cornflour
½ x 185g can crab, drained
½ x 230g can bamboo shoots, finely chopped
plain flour
oil for deep frying
BATTER
⅔ cup plain flour
⅔ cup cornflour
2 teaspoons baking powder
½ cup milk
½ cup water

Remove and discard mushroom stems. Combine pork with soy sauce, sugar and cornflour, stir in crab and bamboo shoots. Place into cavity of mushrooms, mound filling in the centre. Coat mushrooms with flour, dip in batter. Deep fry mushrooms, a few at a time, in hot oil for about 5 minutes or until mushrooms are cooked through and golden brown.

Batter: Sift dry ingredients into bowl, make a well in centre, gradually stir in milk and water, mix to a smooth batter.
   Makes about 36.

RIGHT: Crab-Stuffed Mushrooms.
OPPOSITE PAGE: Oysters with Barbecued Pork.

China from Dansab Pty. Ltd., Sydney; marble table from Burlington Centre, Sydney.

OYSTERS WITH BARBECUED PORK

Prepare topping one day ahead if desired. Keep covered in refrigerator.

30 oysters in shell
185g barbecued pork, finely chopped
4 green shallots, finely chopped
1 teaspoon grated fresh ginger
1 clove garlic, crushed
2 teaspoons light soy sauce
Combine pork, shallots, ginger, garlic and soy sauce in bowl, stand 1 hour. Divide mixture over oysters, grill until heated through.
Makes 30.

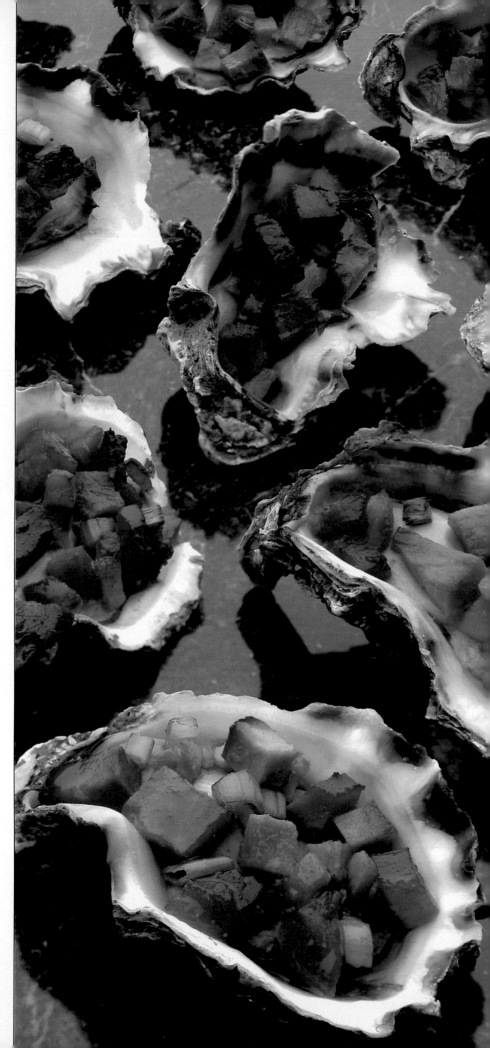

SESAME BEEF BALLS

Balls can be made and shaped up to a day before required. Keep covered in refrigerator. Or, uncooked balls can be frozen for up to two months. Thaw in refrigerator overnight.

500g scotch fillet steak
4 dried mushrooms
1 onion, grated
1 carrot, grated
2 green shallots, finely chopped
2 teaspoons dark soy sauce
2 teaspoons light soy sauce
1 clove garlic, crushed
¾ cup (90g) sesame seeds
oil for deep frying
SAUCE
2 teaspoons tomato sauce
1 tablespoon oil
1 tablespoon dry sherry
1 tablespoon light soy sauce

Cover mushrooms with boiling water, cover, stand 20 minutes; drain. Remove and discard stalks, chop mushroom caps finely. Mince or process steak, add onion, carrot, shallots, mushrooms, sauces and garlic, mix well. Roll teaspoonfuls of mixture into balls, roll in sesame seeds. Deep fry balls in hot oil for about 3 minutes, or until cooked through; drain on absorbent paper. Heat Sauce in wok, add balls and toss until well coated.
Sauce: Combine all ingredients.
Makes about 30.

CHINESE MIXED VEGETABLES

Vegetables will keep in refrigerator, covered, for up to four weeks. Use coarse cooking salt for best results.

¼ cabbage
2 carrots
2 cucumbers
1 small piece (125g) broccoli
4 tablespoons salt
1 cup boiling water
2.5cm piece fresh ginger, sliced
1 tablespoon black peppercorns
1¾ litres (7 cups) cold water
2 tablespoons gin

Cut cabbage into 5cm x 2.5cm pieces, cut carrots into sticks; cut cucumbers lengthwise, remove seeds; cut cucumbers into thick strips; cut broccoli into small flowerets. Wash all vegetables; drain, spread on absorbent paper on wire rack for several hours to dry. Place vegetables in a large jar. Dissolve salt in boiling water, add ginger, peppercorns, cold water and gin, mix well; pour over vegetables, making sure vegetables are completely covered. Stand vegetables at least 5 days before using.

Makes about 1½ litres (6 cups).

FISH AND HAM PUFFS

Puffs can be prepared up to several hours in advance. Uncooked puffs can be frozen for up to two months. Thaw in refrigerator overnight.

375g packet puff pastry
2 white fish fillets
125g ham
3 green shallots, chopped
2 teaspoons dark soy sauce
2 teaspoons dry sherry
4 canned water chestnuts, finely chopped
1 egg, lightly beaten
oil for deep frying

STEP 1

Roll out half the thawed pastry thinly on lightly floured surface; cut out 8cm rounds with sharp cutter. Process fish, ham, shallots, soy sauce and sherry until smooth; stir in water chestnuts. Place teaspoonfuls of mixture onto pastry rounds. Brush around edge with egg, fold over to enclose filling.

STEP 2

Roll and fold edges over. Heat oil in wok, deep fry puffs few minutes, or until golden brown and cooked through; drain on absorbent paper.

Makes about 24.

STUFFED CHICKEN WINGS

Wings can be prepared up to a day before cooking if desired. Stuffed wings can also be wrapped and frozen for up to two weeks. Thaw overnight in refrigerator before frying.

12 chicken wings
250g green prawns, shelled
60g ham, finely chopped
1 teaspoon grated fresh ginger
1 teaspoon sesame seeds
½ teaspoon cornflour
½ teaspoon sugar
1 teaspoon dry sherry
2 tablespoons light soy sauce
¼ teaspoon five spice powder
1 teaspoon honey

Devein prawns; chop finely. Combine prawns, ham, ginger, sesame seeds, cornflour, sugar and sherry.

STEP 1

Cut the small drumsticks off the wings, leaving the middle piece and wing top intact. (Use the drumstick for Sate Chicken Drums at right.)

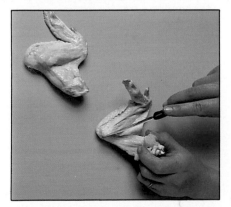

STEP 2

Twist the wing at the joint between the middle piece, scrape meat away with a small sharp knife; do not break the skin. Pull away bone.

STEP 3

Fill bone cavity with teaspoonfuls of prawn mixture. Combine soy sauce, five spice powder and honey; brush mixture over chicken wings; deep fry in hot oil about 5 minutes, or until wings are golden brown.

SATE CHICKEN DRUMS

(See Stuffed Chicken Wings at left).

12 chicken drums
½ cup honey
1 tablespoon brown vinegar
3 tablespoons tomato sauce
½ cup light soy sauce
3 tablespoons sate sauce
¼ cup dry sherry
2 teaspoons grated fresh ginger

Drop chicken into boiling water, cook 10 minutes; drain. Combine remaining ingredients in bowl, add chicken and stir until well coated with marinade; stand 1 hour, turn occasionally. Place chicken and marinade in baking dish, bake in moderate oven 45 minutes, turning chicken frequently.

TOP: Left: Sate Chicken Drums; right: Stuffed Chicken Wings.
OPPOSITE PAGE: Back, from left: Chinese Mixed Vegetables, Sesame Beef Balls; front: Fish and Ham Puffs.

CHINESE SEAFOOD LUNCH FOR FOUR

SEAFOOD WITH NOODLES

SPICY SEAFOOD IN POTATO BASKETS

SWEET AND SOUR FISH

CRAB AND BEAN SPROUT OMELETS

KIWI FRUIT AND GINGER ICE

This menu is light and delicious, and not too time consuming to prepare. There is the usual last minute cooking, but quite a lot of the preparation can be done in advance. We suggest you serve the Seafood Baskets and the Omelets at the one time; a guest might like to cook the Omelets at the table in an electric fry pan while the fish for the third course is baking in the oven. The remaining main course dish is a simple stir-fried recipe.

SEAFOOD WITH NOODLES
250g fresh or frozen egg noodles
500g green king prawns
500g squid
2 tablespoons oil
3 green shallots, finely chopped
1 clove garlic, crushed
½ teaspoon finely chopped chilli
1 red pepper, finely chopped
½ teaspoon grated fresh ginger
SAUCE
1 tablespoon cornflour
½ cup water
¼ cup dry sherry
1 teaspoon light soy sauce
Add noodles to large pan of boiling water, boil uncovered 3 minutes or until tender. Drain, rinse under hot water, spread on absorbent paper.

Shell and devein prawns. Clean squid, cut into rings. Heat oil in wok, add shallots, garlic, chilli, pepper and ginger, stir-fry 1 minute. Add prawns, squid and Sauce, stir until mixture boils and thickens. Add egg noodles, toss until heated through.
Sauce: Blend cornflour and water in pan, add sherry and soy sauce. Stir constantly over heat until Sauce boils and thickens.

In descending order: Sweet and Sour Fish, Seafood with Noodles, Spicy Seafood in Potato Baskets.

SPICY SEAFOOD IN POTATO BASKETS

Potato Baskets can be made, cooled, wrapped tightly in foil or plastic wrap. Store in dry place for up to four days. Reheat about 10 minutes in moderate oven when ready to serve. We used a special double basket for making the Potato Baskets (available from kitchenware shops), however two metal strainers (about 7cm and 9cm) can be used. We used ling fish fillets.

500g white fish fillets
500g green king prawns
250g scallops
250g snow peas
2 tablespoons oil
2 teaspoons grated fresh ginger
1 red pepper, chopped
2 tablespoons hoisin sauce
2 teaspoons sate sauce
POTATO BASKETS
200g old potatoes
¼ cup cornflour
oil for deep frying
Cut fish into bite-sized pieces, shell prawns leaving tails intact; devein prawns and scallops. Top and tail snow peas. Heat oil in wok, add fish, scallops and ginger, stir-fry 2 minutes. Add prawns, pepper and snow peas, stir-fry until prawns are tender. Stir in sauces, spoon into hot Potato Baskets.

STEP 1
Potato Baskets: Peel potatoes, grate potatoes coarsely, rinse under cold water; drain well, combine with cornflour. Brush double strainer lightly with oil, press about quarter of the potato mixture evenly into bottom strainer.

STEP 2
Press top strainer onto potato in bottom strainer. Lower into hot oil, holding handles firmly together, fry until potato is browned; drain well, carefully remove strainers. Repeat with remaining potato to make four Baskets, keep warm in moderate oven.

SWEET AND SOUR FISH

The sauce for this dish can be made the day before required, covered, refrigerated and reheated to serve.

1 whole snapper (about 1kg)
1 egg, lightly beaten
¼ cup cornflour
⅓ cup oil
1 large carrot
1 small green pepper
1 onion
1 tablespoon oil, extra
3 teaspoons cornflour, extra
¾ cup water
1 teaspoon light soy sauce
2 tablespoons tomato sauce
2 tablespoons sugar
1½ tablespoons brown vinegar
2 green shallots, chopped
Clean and scale fish, brush all over outside with egg, dust with cornflour. Heat oil in wok, add fish, fry gently on both sides until golden brown; discard oil. Transfer fish to greased baking dish, bake in moderate oven about 20 minutes or until fish is just tender, turn once after about 10 minutes.

Cut carrot, pepper and onion into thin strips. Heat extra oil in wok, add carrot and onion, stir-fry 3 minutes, add pepper, stir-fry 2 minutes. Blend extra cornflour with combined water, sauces, sugar and vinegar, add to wok, stir until mixture boils and thickens, pour over fish, sprinkle with shallots.

KIWI FRUIT AND GINGER ICE

Ice may be made up to two days before required if desired.

⅓ cup sugar
1 cup water
4 kiwi fruit, peeled
2 tablespoons Green Ginger Wine

Combine sugar and water in pan, stir over heat without boiling until sugar is dissolved, bring to boil, boil 10 minutes uncovered, without stirring; cool to room temperature.

Blend or process kiwi fruit until smooth; strain to remove most of the seeds. Add kiwi fruit to syrup with Ginger Wine. Pour into lamington tin, cover with foil, freeze 1 hour or until almost set. Place mixture into small bowl of electric mixer or processor, beat or process until smooth. Pour back into lamington tin, cover, freeze several hours or overnight.

CRAB AND BEAN SPROUT OMELETS

4 eggs
185g can crab, drained
2 cups bean sprouts
6 green shallots, finely chopped
1 teaspoon grated fresh ginger
SAUCE
1 tablespoon cornflour
1 cup water
1 teaspoon sesame oil
1 tablespoon light soy sauce
½ teaspoon sugar

Beat eggs with whisk until light and frothy, mix in crab, bean sprouts, shallots and ginger.

Lightly oil base of a small pan, heat pan, add quarter of the Omelet mixture. Cook until set on one side, turn, cook other side (see picture below). Transfer to serving plate, cook remaining Omelets. Serve with Sauce.

Sauce: Blend cornflour with water in pan, add remaining ingredients. Stir over heat until Sauce boils and thickens; simmer 1 minute.

TOP: Crab and Bean Sprout Omelets.
RIGHT: Kiwi Fruit and Ginger Ice.

Waterlilies from Ledora Farm, Sydney; plates are Siena by Villeroy & Boch; glass dishes are Accent by Orrefors.

INDIA

Not always searingly hot, more often a titillation for palates seeking the adventure of spices and chilli-by-choice, Indian cooking provides great satisfaction for those who enjoy experimenting with strange and wonderful ingredients.

INDIAN
HOT-AS-YOU-LIKE-IT DINNER PARTY FOR SIX

SPICY TOMATO SOUP

TANDOORI-STYLE CHICKEN AND LAMB

VEGETABLES WITH COCONUT CREAM

LEMON COCONUT RICE

ORANGE JELLY MOUSSE

We have kept the chilli content in this dinner party low so you can adjust it to suit your family's or guests' tastes. The soup and dessert can be made the day before required, and most of the preparation for the main courses can be done beforehand. Last minute cooking of the chicken and lamb, vegetable and rice dishes gives the tastiest results.

SPICY TOMATO SOUP

Make soup the day before to allow maximum flavor development.

15g ghee
2 onions, finely chopped
1 teaspoon yellow mustard seeds
few dried curry leaves
1 teaspoon chilli powder
2 cloves garlic, crushed
¼ cup tomato paste
1 tablespoon sugar
2 tablespoons plain flour
2 cups chicken stock
400g can tomatoes
1kg tomatoes, peeled, chopped

Heat ghee in pan, add onions, cook onions until light golden brown. Add mustard seeds, curry leaves and chilli powder, cook 1 minute while stirring. Add garlic, tomato paste, sugar and flour, cook 1 minute while stirring. Gradually stir in stock, crushed, undrained canned tomatoes and fresh tomatoes; bring to boil, cover, reduce heat, simmer 1 hour, stirring occasionally. Serve soup with about a tablespoon of cream in each bowl if desired.

LEMON COCONUT RICE

2 cups rice
½ teaspoon turmeric
30g ghee
1 onion, finely chopped
½ teaspoon yellow mustard seeds
½ teaspoon chilli powder
few dried curry leaves
1 teaspoon coarsely grated lemon rind
2 cloves garlic, crushed
½ cup canned coconut milk
¼ cup lemon juice
½ cup shredded coconut

Cook rice in boiling water with turmeric for 8 minutes; drain, rinse under cold water; drain well. Heat ghee in large pan, add onion, cook, stirring until light golden brown. Add mustard seeds, chilli powder and curry leaves, cook, stirring 1 minute, add rice, cook, stirring few minutes. Stir in lemon rind, garlic, coconut milk and lemon juice; bring to boil, reduce heat, simmer, covered, 10 minutes or until rice is tender. Place coconut on oven tray, toast in moderate oven for about 3 minutes. Stir coconut into rice before serving.

Back, from left: Spicy Tomato Soup, Lemon Coconut Rice; front, from left: Tandoori-Style Chicken and Lamb, Vegetables with Coconut Cream.

Background cloth and copper soup pot from Gallery Nomad, Paddington, NSW.

KEY TO PREVIOUS PAGE

1 brown mustard seeds
2 yellow mustard seeds
3 brown lentils
4 red lentils
5 urid dahl
6 chick peas
7 short grain rice
8 brown rice
9 basmati rice
10 fresh green and red chillies
11 sesame seeds
12 tandoori color
13 turmeric
14 paprika
15 fresh ginger
16 dried chillies
17 ground chillies
18 black sesame seeds
19 almonds
20 cashews
21 pistachio nuts
22 garlic
23 caraway seeds
24 curry powder
25 fresh curry leaves
26 cumin seeds
27 coriander
28 saffron threads
29 cinnamon sticks
30 mint
31 dried curry leaves
32 black cumin seeds
33 ground coriander
34 ground saffron
35 ground cinnamon
36 fresh coriander
37 ground cumin
38 garam masala
39 cardamom pods
40 cardamom seeds
41 coconut
42 shredded coconut
43 pappadams
44 ground cardamom

TANDOORI-STYLE CHICKEN AND LAMB

Chicken and lamb can be combined with the yoghurt mixture, covered and refrigerated the day before required.

6 boned chicken thighs, (skin on)
6 lamb cutlets
⅔ cup plain yoghurt
2 cloves garlic, crushed
2 teaspoons garam masala
1 teaspoon ground cardamom
1 teaspoon chilli powder
tiny pinch saffron powder
1 teaspoon paprika
few drops red food coloring
YOGHURT DRESSING
1 cup plain yoghurt
1 tablespoon chopped fresh coriander
1 tablespoon chopped mint
1 teaspoon chilli powder

Trim away any excess fat from chicken and lamb. Combine yoghurt with garlic, garam masala, cardamom and chilli. Spoon half this mixture into a bowl, stir in saffron; add chicken, mix well. Place remaining half of mixture into another bowl, stir in paprika and coloring; add lamb, mix well. Marinate chicken and lamb at least 1 hour (or, refrigerate, covered, overnight). Place chicken and lamb on rack over baking dish. Bake in very hot oven 10 minutes or until tender; it is not necessary to turn the meat during cooking. Cut into bite-sized pieces if desired before serving with Yoghurt Dressing.
Yoghurt Dressing: Combine all ingredients and mix thoroughly.

VEGETABLES WITH COCONUT CREAM

1 medium eggplant
3 medium zucchini
1 red pepper
1 green pepper
3 medium carrots
250g green beans
1 piece (300g) pumpkin
60g ghee
2 tablespoons oil
2 cloves garlic, crushed
1 small fresh red chilli, finely chopped
2 teaspoons black mustard seeds
2 teaspoons yellow mustard seeds
2 teaspoons cumin seeds
1 cup canned coconut cream
1 cup plain yoghurt

Cut all vegetables into thin 6cm strips. Heat ghee and oil in large pan, add garlic, chilli, mustard and cumin seeds, cook, stirring 1 minute. Add vegetables, cook, stirring a few minutes or until vegetables are just tender; add coconut cream and yoghurt, stir until heated through.

BELOW: Orange Jelly Mousse

Peacock statuette from Indian Tourist Office, Sydney.

ORANGE JELLY MOUSSE

This is a light refreshing dessert ideal to serve after spicy foods. The layers sometimes change place during the setting time; don't worry if this happens. Any type of orange juice can be used for this recipe; strain before using for a clearer jelly. Mousse can be made a day before required.

1 cup orange juice
⅓ cup sugar
3 teaspoons gelatine
½ cup dry white wine
300ml carton thickened cream
1½ cups orange juice, extra
3 tablespoons sugar, extra
2 teaspoons gelatine, extra
⅓ cup dry white wine, extra

Combine orange juice, sugar and gelatine in pan, stir over heat, without boiling until sugar and gelatine is dissolved. Remove from heat, add wine, pour into bowl, cool, refrigerate until set to the consistency of unbeaten egg white. Lightly fold in whipped cream. Pour into six individual wetted moulds (1 cup capacity), refrigerate until set. While this layer is setting, prepare jelly layer. Combine extra orange juice, extra sugar and extra gelatine in pan, stir over heat without boiling until sugar and gelatine is dissolved. Remove from heat, add extra wine, cool to room temperature. Pour over first layer, refrigerate several hours or overnight before removing mould.

INDIAN TANGY BARBECUE FOR EIGHT

FISH CUTLETS WITH CHUTNEY GLAZE

TASTY CHEESE PARATHAS

SPICY BEEF STICKS

CHICK PEA AND TOMATO SALAD

PRAWNS WITH HOT PEANUT SAUCE

ALMOND DIAMONDS

Barbecues are a flamboyant way of entertaining summer or winter — try some Indian-style food for a change. Indians usually serve the hottest food in the hottest months. These recipes are ideal for all seasons.

FISH CUTLETS WITH CHUTNEY GLAZE

Marinate fish in chutney glaze overnight if desired. Keep covered and refrigerated. We used snapper cutlets.

8 white fish cutlets or steaks
2 tablespoons mango chutney
2 teaspoons grated fresh ginger
2 tablespoons oil
1 teaspoon garam masala
1 teaspoon ground cumin
¼ teaspoon chilli powder
2 tablespoons lime juice
2 cloves garlic, crushed
1 mango, chopped
200g carton plain yoghurt
1 teaspoon grated fresh ginger, extra

Combine chutney, ginger, oil, garam masala, cumin, chilli, lime juice and garlic in bowl, mix well, spread over both sides of fish cutlets; stand 30 minutes at room temperature.

Barbecue or grill until browned on both sides and cooked through, baste with remaining mixture as it cooks. Puree mango in processor, place in bowl with yoghurt and extra ginger, mix well, serve as a sauce.

ABOVE: Fish Cutlets with Chutney Glaze.

Banana leaves from Florida Garden Centre, Blakehurst, NSW.

41

TASTY CHEESE PARATHAS

2 cups plain wholemeal flour
2 cups plain white flour
60g ghee
1 cup warm water
1 cup mashed potato
2 cups (200g) grated tasty cheese
2 tablespoons cumin seeds
2 tablespoons coriander seeds
extra ghee for frying

Sift flours into bowl, return husks from sifter to bowl. Rub in ghee, add water, mix to a firm dough. Knead on lightly floured surface for 5 minutes or until smooth. Cover, stand 10 minutes. Combine potato, cheese and spices in bowl; mix well.

STEP 1

Divide dough into 8 portions, press each portion into a round with hands.

STEP 2

Place a tablespoonful of potato mixture onto each round. Gather edges to enclose filling.

STEP 3

Roll into a ball, then roll out to a 10cm circle. Melt extra ghee in pan or on barbecue plate, cook each side until crisp and golden brown.

SPICY BEEF STICKS

You will need ⅓ cup uncooked rice for this recipe. Meat mixture can be prepared and refrigerated the day before required. The uncooked mixture can be wrapped and frozen for up to three months if desired.

500g topside steak
1 onion
1 cup cooked rice
½ teaspoon ground coriander
½ teaspoon ground cumin
½ teaspoon chilli powder
½ teaspoon garam masala
2 tablespoons fruit chutney

Trim fat from steak, mince or process steak and onion finely; mix in rice and spices. Divide mixture into 8, roll each portion into sausage shapes, insert skewers lengthways through centres. Barbecue or grill, turning frequently, until brown, brush with a little chutney towards end of cooking time.

CHICK PEA AND TOMATO SALAD

Salad can be made, covered and refrigerated a day before required.

2 cups dry chick peas (garbanzos)
4 tomatoes, peeled, chopped
2 onions, finely chopped
DRESSING
¼ cup lemon juice
2 tablespoons chopped fresh mint
2 cloves garlic, crushed
1 tablespoon grated fresh ginger
1 small finely chopped fresh red chilli
1 teaspoon sugar

Soak chick peas in water overnight.
Next day: Drain peas, rinse, place in pan, cover with water, cover, bring to boil, reduce heat, simmer about 1 hour or until just tender. Drain, rinse under cold water, drain well, cool to room temperature.
Combine chick peas, tomatoes, onion and Dressing.
Dressing: Combine all ingredients.

LEFT: Clockwise from front: Prawns with Hot Peanut Sauce, Spicy Beef Sticks, Tasty Cheese Parathas, Chick Pea and Tomato Salad, Fish Cutlets with Chutney Glaze.

Tiles from Fred Pazotti Pty. Ltd., Woollahra, NSW; bougainvillea plant from The Flower Man, Double Bay, NSW.

PRAWNS WITH HOT PEANUT SAUCE

Hot Peanut Sauce can be made several days in advance. Prawns can be cooked in a pan or wok over the barbecue or on a solid plate.

1kg green king prawns
1 small onion, finely chopped
2 cloves garlic, crushed
1 teaspoon grated fresh ginger
1 tablespoon lemon juice
1 tablespoon oil
½ teaspoon finely chopped fresh red chilli
½ teaspoon turmeric
¼ teaspoon ground coriander
¼ teaspoon ground cumin
15g ghee
HOT PEANUT SAUCE
15g ghee
1 onion, finely chopped
1 teaspoon garam masala
½ teaspoon chilli powder
1 teaspoon ground cumin
1 clove garlic, crushed
1 teaspoon grated fresh ginger
½ cup crunchy peanut butter
¾ cup water
½ cup canned coconut milk
1 tablespoon lemon juice

Shell prawns, leave tails intact. Split prawns lengthways in half, still attached at tail, remove vein. Combine onion, garlic, ginger, lemon juice, oil, chilli, turmeric, coriander and cumin in bowl; mix well, stir in prawns; marinate 30 minutes.

Heat ghee in large pan, add prawn mixture, cook, stirring, until prawns are just tender. Serve with Sauce.

Hot Peanut Sauce: Heat ghee in pan, add onion, cook, stirring, until onion is golden brown. Add garam masala, chilli and cumin, cook 1 minute, stirring, stir in garlic, ginger, peanut butter, water, coconut milk and lemon juice. Bring to boil, reduce heat, simmer 5 minutes.

ALMOND DIAMONDS

Mixture can be prepared up to two hours before baking.

½ cup ground almonds
1¾ cups skim milk powder
1 cup castor sugar
tiny pinch saffron powder
few drops almond essence
125g unsalted butter, melted
3 eggs, lightly beaten

Combine almonds, milk powder, sugar and saffron in bowl. Stir in almond essence and butter, then eggs. Pour into greased and base-lined square 20cm cake tin. Bake in moderately slow oven 40 minutes or until golden brown. Turn out, cut into diamonds, serve hot, dusted with icing sugar and topped with extra toasted almond kernels.

LEFT: Almond Diamonds.

CHILLI VEGETABLE PATTIES

SPICED PUMPKIN

LENTIL AND VEGETABLE CASSEROLE

CURRIED YOGHURT RICE

CARROT CREAM DESSERT

INDIAN VEGETARIAN DINNER PARTY FOR FOUR

A large number of Indians — and people from neighboring countries — never eat meat because of religious beliefs, or they eat it rarely or in small quantities due to scarcity. By using different combinations of herbs and spices with vegetables they create wonderful tasting dishes. The recipes we've chosen are substantial and full of robust flavor — you might be surprised when your family or guests don't notice the absence of meat.

CARROT CREAM DESSERT

This dish can be made the day before required and refrigerated. Serve with a selection of fresh fruit.

3 medium (375g) carrots, finely grated
4 cups (1 litre) milk
⅓ cup sugar
⅔ cup raisins
30g butter
tiny pinch saffron powder
Combine carrots and milk in pan, bring to boil, reduce heat, simmer 30 minutes or until milk is reduced by half. Add sugar, raisins, butter and saffron, cook for about 10 minutes, stirring occasionally, until raisins are plump. Spoon into serving dishes, serve warm or cold sprinkled with shelled pistachio nuts if desired.

RIGHT: Carrot Cream Dessert.

Cloth from Gallery Nomad, Paddington, NSW.

CHILLI VEGETABLE PATTIES

Use any chutney of your choice to accompany this recipe.

4 large potatoes
30g ghee
1 cup grated tasty cheese
plain flour
2 eggs, lightly beaten
packaged breadcrumbs
ghee for frying
FILLING
1 carrot
1 zucchini, peeled
1 small red pepper
1 small green pepper
1 small onion
1 stick celery
30g ghee
1 clove garlic, crushed
1 small fresh red chilli, finely
    chopped
2 teaspoons yellow mustard seeds
2 teaspoons coriander seeds
¼ cup water
2 teaspoons plain flour
⅔ cup chutney

STEP 1

Boil or steam potatoes until tender; drain, mash well with ghee, stir in cheese; cool to room temperature. Shape a tablespoon of potato mixture into a patty shape, top with a tablespoon of Filling.

STEP 2

Place another tablespoon of potato mixture on Filling, mould potato around Filling to seal completely; shape into patties. Coat lightly with flour, dip in eggs, then breadcrumbs. Heat ghee in pan, fry patties until golden brown.

Filling: Chop all vegetables finely. Heat ghee in pan, add garlic, chilli and spices, cook 1 minute, stirring. Add vegetables, stir 5 minutes or until vegetables are soft. Stir in blended water, flour and chutney, stir constantly until mixture boils and thickens; cool to room temperature before using.

Makes 4.

SPICED PUMPKIN

1kg pumpkin, peeled, cubed
60g ghee
2 teaspoons ground cumin
1 teaspoon garam masala
2 cloves garlic, crushed
2 tablespoons chopped chives

Boil, steam or microwave pumpkin until almost tender; drain well (if pumpkin is moist, pat dry with absorbent paper). Heat ghee in pan, add cumin and garam masala, cook, stirring, 1 minute, add pumpkin, cook until golden brown all over. Stir in garlic and chives just before serving.

LENTIL AND VEGETABLE CASSEROLE

This dish can be cooked and refrigerated the day before required.

250g broccoli
60g ghee
1 onion, chopped
2 cloves garlic, crushed
1 teaspoon curry powder
½ teaspoon garam masala
1½ cups red lentils
2 potatoes, chopped
2 carrots, sliced
4 cups water

Cut broccoli into small flowerets. Heat ghee in pan, add onion and garlic, cook, stirring, until onion is soft. Add curry and garam masala, cook 1 minute, stirring. Add lentils, potatoes, carrots and water, cover, bring to boil, reduce heat, simmer 10 minutes. Stir in broccoli, simmer 10 minutes or until the vegetables are tender.

Back, from left: Spiced Pumpkin, Lentil and Vegetable Casserole, Carrot Cream Dessert; front, from left: Curried Yoghurt Rice, Chilli Vegetable Patties.

CURRIED YOGHURT RICE

Reserve water from boiled or steamed vegetables to make the stock.

15g ghee
1 onion, finely chopped
2 teaspoons curry powder
1 clove garlic, crushed
2 cups brown rice
4 cups vegetable stock
½ cup dry white wine
tiny pinch saffron powder
200g carton plain yoghurt
1 teaspoon chopped fresh coriander

Heat ghee in pan, add onion, cook, stirring, until light golden brown, add curry powder, garlic and rice, cook, stirring, 2 minutes or until rice is opaque. Add stock, wine and saffron to pan, bring to the boil, reduce heat, cover with tight-fitting lid, simmer over very low heat 30 minutes or until liquid is absorbed and rice tender. Stir in yoghurt and coriander before serving.

INDIAN BUFFET FOR 10

A curry party is a popular way to entertain people, although it is always wise to check if your guests like hot spicy food. Serve the Samosas first, then the main course dishes with the rice and Sambals. Serve the Dip with whatever fresh fruits are in season.

Clockwise from front: Beef and Vegetable Samosas, Sambals, Pappadams, Chicken Curry with Coconut Cream, Masala Lamb, Fruit and Nut Rice; centre: Peach and Mint Relish.

Copper dishes in right hand corner from Berczi Copper, Sydney; cloth and other copper dishes and platter from Gallery Nomad, Paddington, NSW; painting from Indian Tourist Office Sydney; frangipani plant from The Flower Man, Double Bay, NSW.

BEEF AND VEGETABLE SAMOSAS

CHICKEN CURRY WITH COCONUT CREAM

MASALA LAMB

FRUIT AND NUT RICE

SAMBALS

PAPPADAMS

YOGHURT MANGO FRUIT DIP

BEEF AND VEGETABLE SAMOSAS

Serve these tasty morsels with a bowl of your favourite chutney

PASTRY
3 cups plain flour
60g ghee
2 tablespoons cumin seeds
1 cup warm water, approximately
oil for deep frying
FILLING
300g minced beef
60g ghee
1 small onion, finely chopped
1 clove garlic, crushed
1 tablespoon grated fresh ginger
1 tablespoon cumin seeds
1 tablespoon coriander seeds
2 tablespoons garam masala
1 tablespoon turmeric
1 tablespoon chilli powder
1 large potato, finely chopped
1 cup fresh or frozen peas
1 cup water
1 tablespoon plain flour
¼ cup water, extra

STEP 1
Pastry: Sift flour into bowl, rub in ghee, add cumin, gradually stir in enough water to mix to a firm dough. Knead on lightly floured surface for about 5 minutes or until smooth. Cover, stand 10 minutes. Divide pastry in half, roll each half to 3mm thickness. Cut into rounds using 9cm cutter. Place a teaspoonful of Filling into centre of each round, brush edges of pastry lightly with water before folding in half.

BELOW: Back from left: Mango and Apple Relish, Cucumber and Carrot Shred, Peach and Mint Relish; front from left: Peppers with Lemon, Coconut Ginger Sambal, Green Bean Sambal.

STEP 2
Press edges together with thumb and finger, as shown. Repeat with remaining Pastry and Filling.
Heat oil in pan, deep fry Samosas a few at a time until golden brown; drain on absorbent paper.

Filling: Heat ghee in pan, add onion, garlic, ginger and spices, cook 1 minute, stirring. Add beef, cook, while stirring, 5 minutes, add potatoes, peas and water, bring to the boil, reduce heat, simmer, covered, 20 minutes or until potatoes are tender. Blend flour with extra water, add to pan, stir until mixture boils and thickens. Cool to room temperature before using.

CHICKEN CURRY WITH COCONUT CREAM

Curry can be made the day before required. Chicken mixture can be frozen for up to two months, add yoghurt mixture after thawing and reheating.

2kg chicken thigh fillets
¾ cup plain flour
3 teaspoons ground cumin
¼ cup oil
60g ghee
3 onions, chopped
1 teaspoon garam masala
1 teaspoon curry powder
1 teaspoon ground cumin, extra
1 clove garlic, crushed
1 teaspoon grated fresh ginger
1 tablespoon sugar
4 cups chicken stock
200ml carton plain yoghurt
½ cup canned coconut cream
2 tablespoons lemon juice

Cut chicken into pieces. Combine flour and cumin in bag, shake well. Add chicken to bag in batches, shake off excess flour. Heat oil in large pan, add chicken to pan in single layer, stir over high heat until well browned all over, remove from pan. Repeat process with remaining chicken.

Clean pan, add ghee, heat; add onions, cook, stirring until light golden brown. Add garam masala, curry powder and extra cumin, cook 1 minute, stirring; add garlic, ginger and sugar, cook further 1 minute, stirring. Return chicken to pan with chicken stock, bring to the boil, cover, reduce heat, simmer 1 hour, stirring occasionally. (If preferred, chicken can be cooked in an overproof dish in a moderate oven for 1 hour). Stir combined yoghurt, coconut cream and lemon juice into chicken, reheat without boiling.

MASALA LAMB

Ask the butcher to bone the lamb for you. This curry improves in flavor if refrigerated one to two days before required. It will also freeze well for up to three months.

2 x 2kg legs of lamb, boned
½ cup oil
3 large onions, chopped
4 tomatoes, peeled, chopped
1 cup water
2 tablespoons cornflour
2 tablespoons water, extra
MASALA PASTE
1 cup fresh coriander leaves
1 cup fresh mint leaves
2 cloves garlic, crushed
2 teaspoons grated fresh ginger
2 teaspoons curry powder
1½ teaspoons chilli powder
½ teaspoon ground cardamom
¼ cup white vinegar

Trim fat from lamb, cut lamb into cubes. Heat half the oil in a large pan, add onions, cook, stirring until light golden brown; remove from pan. Heat remaining oil in pan, add lamb gradually to pan. Do not have more than a single layer of lamb in the pan at the one time or lamb will stew, not brown. Cook, stirring, over high heat until lamb is well browned all over. Repeat process with remaining lamb. Return onion and lamb to pan with tomatoes, water and Masala Paste, bring to boil, cover, reduce heat, simmer 45 minutes or until lamb is tender. Blend cornflour with extra water, stir into lamb mixture, stir until mixture boils and thickens.
Masala Paste: Blend or process all ingredients until smooth.

ABOVE RIGHT: Back: Masala Lamb; front: Fruit and Nut Rice.

FRUIT AND NUT RICE

Basmati rice is a beautifully flavored type of long grain rice.

1kg basmati rice
90g ghee
2 tablespoons oil
2 cloves garlic, crushed
1 onion, finely chopped
1 tablespoon cumin seeds
1 tablespoon caraway seeds
1 tablespoon coriander seeds
6 cardamom seeds
1 cinnamon stick
4 cups (1 litre) hot water
tiny pinch saffron powder
¾ cup chopped dried apricots
1 cup sultanas
1 cup roasted unsalted cashews
½ cup chopped pistachio nuts

Wash rice; drain 30 minutes. Heat ghee and oil in large pan, add garlic, onion and spices, cook, stirring, 1 minute. Add rice, stir until rice is coated with ghee, stir in combined water and saffron. Bring to the boil, cover with tight-fitting lid, reduce heat to very low, steam 20 minutes or until water is absorbed and rice is tender. Add apricots and sultanas, cover, cook over low heat 10 minutes, stir in cashews, serve sprinkled with pistachios.

SAMBALS
PAPPADAMS
20 pappadams
Deep fry one at a time in hot oil for about 10 seconds or until golden brown and puffed; drain.

PEACH AND MINT RELISH
1 cup mint leaves
1 onion, finely chopped
¼ cup lemon juice
½ teaspoon garam masala
2 tablespoons cream
410g can pie peaches
Blend or process all ingredients to a smooth consistency.

GREEN BEAN SAMBAL
250g green beans
1 onion, finely chopped
1 tomato, peeled, chopped
¼ cup oil
¼ cup lemon juice
1 small fresh red chilli, finely chopped
2 teaspoons yellow mustard seeds
1 clove garlic, crushed
Top and tail beans, cut into 3cm pieces, boil, steam or microwave until just tender, cool. Combine beans with remaining ingredients.

MANGO AND APPLE RELISH

2 mangoes, chopped
2 Granny Smith apples, peeled, chopped
½ cup brown sugar
1 cup dry white wine
1 fresh red chilli, finely chopped
1 cinnamon stick

Combine all ingredients in pan, bring to boil, boil 5 minutes, reduce heat, simmer uncovered 20 minutes or until mixture thickens.

CUCUMBER AND CARROT SHRED

1 large cucumber, seeded, grated
1 large carrot, grated
½ cup plain yoghurt

Combine all ingredients.

COCONUT GINGER SAMBAL

1 cup shredded coconut
2 tablespoons grated fresh ginger
1 tablespoon chopped fresh coriander
½ cup canned coconut cream
¼ cup cream
¼ cup plain yoghurt
1 small fresh red chilli, finely chopped

Combine all ingredients, except chilli, mix well. Serve topped with chilli.

PEPPERS WITH LEMON

1 green pepper
1 red pepper
2 tablespoons lemon juice
1 tablespoon toasted sesame seeds

Cut peppers into diamond shapes, mix in lemon juice and sesame seeds.

YOGHURT MANGO FRUIT DIP

1 mango, chopped
200g carton plain yoghurt
½ cup sugar
pinch cinnamon
½ cup toasted slivered almonds

Puree mango in blender or processor until smooth, place mango in bowl with yoghurt, sugar and cinnamon, mix well. Reserve a few toasted almonds; finely chop remaining almonds, stir into the mango mixture. Pour into serving bowl or hollowed-out halved pineapple shells. Sprinkle with reserved almonds, serve with fresh fruit.

BELOW: Yoghurt Mango Fruit Dip.

JAPAN

Japanese is the most delicate and disciplined of cuisines, aesthetically pleasing and dedicated to the artistry of food presentation. Our recipes offer visual elegance and intriguing new taste experiences.

MISO SOUP WITH TOFU

2 x 10g sachets instant dashi powder
6 cups (1½ litres) hot water
2 green shallots
300g carton silken tofu
¼ cup red miso
6 small oyster or abalone mushrooms
alfalfa sprouts

Combine dashi and hot water in pan. Cut shallots into 5cm lengths, then into fine shreds, place into bowl of iced water until shallots curl. Cut tofu into cubes; drain shallots, divide tofu and shallots between six soup bowls. Heat dashi in pan. Place red miso into small sieve, lower into hot dashi, whisk until miso is dissolved. Remove sieve, discard any undissolved miso remaining in sieve, reheat without boiling. Spoon dashi into soup bowls, garnish with alfalfa sprouts, oyster mushrooms, and carrot twists if desired. Serve at once.

ABOVE: Miso Soup with Tofu.
RIGHT: Sukiyaki.

Bowls, pot, egg dish and chopsticks from Japanese Book Shop, The Rocks, Sydney; divided tray and fans from Dansab Pty. Ltd., Chippendale, NSW; burgundy background is Mini-Graph from Formica, Sydney.

Previous page: black background is Graph from Formica, Sydney; plates and dishes from Made in Japan Shop, Mosman, NSW; dashi and wasabi dishes from Dansab. Pty Ltd., Chippendale, NSW.

KEY TO PREVIOUS PAGE

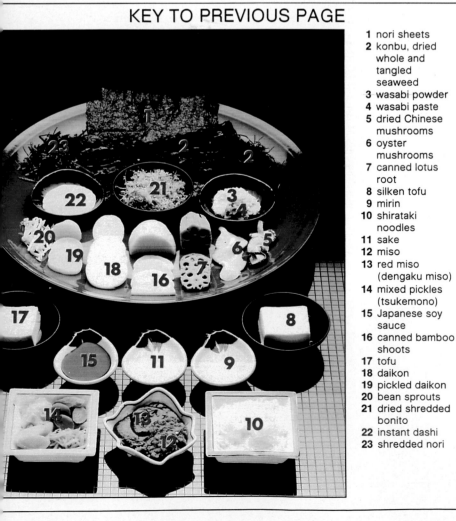

1 nori sheets
2 konbu, dried whole and tangled seaweed
3 wasabi powder
4 wasabi paste
5 dried Chinese mushrooms
6 oyster mushrooms
7 canned lotus root
8 silken tofu
9 mirin
10 shirataki noodles
11 sake
12 miso
13 red miso (dengaku miso)
14 mixed pickles (tsukemono)
15 Japanese soy sauce
16 canned bamboo shoots
17 tofu
18 daikon
19 pickled daikon
20 bean sprouts
21 dried shredded bonito
22 instant dashi
23 shredded nori

SUKIYAKI

A traditional Sukiyaki pan can be purchased from stores which stock Japanese or Asian goods, however, an electric fry pan is a good substitute. Small quantities of Sukiyaki are cooked and served individually to guests. Each guest usually has a small bowl containing an egg which has been lightly beaten with chopsticks; the hot food is dipped into the egg before being eaten. Always serve Sukiyaki with rice. Partly freeze steak before slicing.

750g eye fillet beef steak (in one piece)
12 dried mushrooms
4 tablespoons oil
3 small onions, quartered
2 cups (200g) bean sprouts
½ Chinese cabbage, chopped
1 red pepper, sliced
6 green shallots, chopped
250g tofu, cubed
359g packet shirataki noodles, drained
SAUCE
10g sachet instant dashi powder
1 cup hot water
½ cup Japanese light soy sauce
½ cup mirin
1 tablespoon sugar

Slice steak thinly. Cover mushrooms with hot water, cover, soak 20 minutes; drain, remove and discard stalks. Heat 1 tablespoon of the oil in pan, add about quarter of the steak, stir-fry quickly over high heat until well browned all over. Add quarter of the mushrooms, vegetables, tofu and rinsed noodles to pan, stir-fry quickly over high heat until tender; pour over quarter of the Sauce. Serve at once, repeat with remaining ingredients.
Sauce: Combine all ingredients in pan, stir over heat until sugar is dissolved. Bring to the boil.

JAPANESE WINTER DINNER PARTY FOR SIX

MISO SOUP WITH TOFU

SUKIYAKI

FRESH FRUIT PLATTER

The dishes in this menu are fairly typical of those served in Japan during the cold winter months. The soup is light and nourishing while the Sukiyaki is hearty with a mixture of taste and texture sensations. We served the Sukiyaki with pickled ginger, cucumber and carrot — all of which are available in sachets from stores which stock Asian food. Fresh fruit is a delightful finish to this dinner party.

FRESH FRUIT PLATTER

Here are some simple but attractive ways to present a variety of fruit. Arrange them neatly spaced on a platter.

Orange Segments
Peel orange thickly; using sharp knife, cut down both sides of membrane which joins the segments to release the orange segments.

BELOW: Fresh Fruit Platter.

Tray from Dansab Pty. Ltd., Chippendale, NSW.

Strawberry Butterflies
Step 1
Cut strawberries into fine slices.

Step 2
Place two of the three inside slices on plate, top with the two end pieces of strawberry. Cut feelers from outside edge of remaining slice, place in position at top edge of slices.

Pineapple Cones
Cut thin slices of unpeeled pineapple, cut a small wedge from each slice; twist into cone shape.

Apple Birds
Cut a quarter from the apple, cut the quarter into wedges as shown. Arrange wedges into bird shape.

JAPANESE SUMMER DINNER PARTY FOR FOUR

ABOVE: Sushi.

Background paper, plate and chopsticks from Japanese Book Shop, Sydney.

SUSHI

SQUID SASHIMI

CLEAR SOUP WITH LOBSTER AND SPINACH

TERIYAKI CHICKEN WITH ZUCCHINI SLICES

RICE

SUMMER SALAD

SNOW WHITE STRAWBERRY JELLY

If you've never prepared Japanese food before, this is a good menu with which to start. The step-by-steps will help you gain confidence with this unique style of food. The flavor and texture is light and delicate, and particularly good for the health conscious. Unfamiliar ingredients are explained in our Glossary at the end of the book.

SUSHI

The bamboo mats we used to make the Sushi are inexpensive and are helpful in the rolling process.

2 cups short grain rice
3 cups water
⅓ cup rice vinegar
⅓ cup sugar
3 teaspoons salt
5 sheets nori, toasted
2 teaspoons wasabi paste
FILLINGS
1 small green cucumber, peeled
3 spinach leaves
100g ham
60g packet sliced pickled ginger
2 eggs
2 teaspoons sugar
1 teaspoon salt

STEP 1

Cover rice with cold water, stand for 1 hour; drain well. Combine rice and the 3 cups of water in pan, bring to boil, reduce heat, simmer, uncovered, until water is absorbed. Cover, reduce heat to as low as possible, cook 5 minutes. Allow rice to cool slightly, stir in combined vinegar, sugar and salt.

Toast nori lightly (see note in Squid Sashimi recipe).

STEP 2

Cut a strip about 4cm wide from the narrow end of the nori as shown. Place the large piece of nori in the centre of the bamboo mat, place the extra narrow strip in the centre; this helps strengthen the nori during rolling.

STEP 3

Spread about a fifth of the rice over nori leaving 4cm edge as shown. Make a hollow with fingers as shown. If rice is too sticky, moisten fingers with a little rice vinegar.

STEP 4

Spread wasabi paste along hollow in rice, place a combination of cucumber, spinach and ham in hollow or combination of ginger and omelet in hollow of rice as shown.

STEP 5

Use bamboo mat to help roll the Sushi, pressing firmly as you roll.

STEP 6

Remove bamboo mat, use a sharp knife to cut Sushi into 4cm slices.

Fillings: Slice cucumber in half lengthwise, scoop out seeds, cut cucumber into long narrow strips. Drop spinach leaves into pan of boiling water; drain immediately, press as much water as possible from the spinach leaves; do this between pieces of absorbent paper. Cut ham into fine strips. Beat eggs, sugar and salt together with fork, pour into small greased pan, cook, over medium heat until set. Remove from pan, cool, cut into long fine strips.

SQUID SASHIMI

Wasabi is bought in a paste, or a powder to which water is added to form a paste. Use either one. Nori must be toasted lightly; this can be done by holding the sheets, with tongs, over a flame or by grilling them for a minute or two. Both sides must be toasted until the nori is just crisp. We found the easiest way was to place a sheet at a time on an oven tray, bake in a moderate oven for a minute or two, or until sheets are just crisp; there is no need to turn the nori using this method.

2 tubes squid
2 sheets nori, toasted
4 green shallots
2 tablespoons lime juice
1 tablespoon grated daikon
⅛ teaspoon wasabi paste

STEP 1

Clean squid. Cut open, flatten out on board with outside facing up. Use a sharp knife to make fine incisions lengthways into squid; be careful not to cut right through.

STEP 2

Lightly toast nori. Turn squid over so the scored side is facing downwards. Place one sheet of nori on squid, turn over, trim to same size with scissors.

ABOVE: Squid Sashimi.

China from Made in Japan, Mosman, NSW.

STEP 3
Turn over again so squid is down-wards. Cut shallots into some length as squid, then cut shallots into fine strips. Place half the shallots in row on long side of squid.

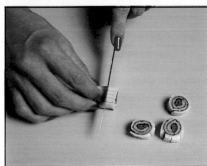

STEP 4
Roll up squid tightly around shallots. Repeat with remaining squid, nori and shallots.

Hold roll with seam downwards, cut into 1cm slices; place into shallow dish. Pour lime juice over rolls, cover, refrigerate several hours or until squid turns opaque, spoon lime juice over squid several times during standing. Serve with grated daikon, topped with wasabi paste.

CLEAR SOUP WITH LOBSTER AND SPINACH

Dashi can be made up to 12 hours in advance. If preferred, instant dashi is sold at Japanese shops.

1 medium green lobster tail
cornflour
50g English spinach (about 8 leaves)
DASHI
4 cups (1 litre) cold water
10g konbu
3 x 4g packets dried bonito flakes

Cut lobster into 1cm slices, roll in cornflour. Poach lobster in pan of boiling salted water for 2 minutes, drain on paper. Add spinach to the same pan of boiling water, reduce heat, simmer 2 minutes. Place drained spinach immediately into bowl of iced water. When spinach is cold, wrap spinach in clean cloth, squeeze out moisture. Cut spinach into 4 × 5cm pieces.

Bring dashi to the boil, season to taste with salt. Divide lobster and spinach between four bowls, add dashi.

Dashi: Place water in pan, add konbu, bring slowly to the boil. Remove konbu just before the water boils, strain through muslin-lined sieve; discard konbu. Add bonito flakes to konbu stock, bring to boil, immediately remove from heat. Allow flakes to settle, strain through muslin-lined sieve.

TERIYAKI CHICKEN WITH ZUCCHINI SLICES

4 chicken thighs, (skin on)
2 tablespoons oil
2 tablespoons Japanese light soy sauce
2 tablespoons sake
1 tablespoon mirin
2 teaspoons sugar
ZUCCHINI SLICES
2 zucchini
1 tablespoon oil
2 teaspoons miso
2 teaspoons sake
1 teaspoon sugar

Make cuts, 1cm apart, through skin and partially into flesh of chicken thighs. Heat oil in pan, fry chicken on each side until brown. Add combined soy sauce, sake, mirin and sugar to pan, stir until chicken is tender and well coated with sauce. Using a sharp knife, cut through thighs completely, serve with Zucchini Slices.

Zucchini Slices: Cut zucchini into diagonal slices. Heat oil in small pan, stir-fry zucchini quickly over high heat until just tender and lightly browned. Stir in combined miso, sake and sugar.

ABOVE: Clear Soup with Lobster and Spinach.
RIGHT: Back: Summer Salad; front: Teriyaki Chicken with Zucchini Slices.

Plates are Grey Crackle from Made in Japan, Mosman, NSW.

SUMMER SALAD

250g bunch asparagus
100g snow peas
½ x 540g can lotus root, drained
½ x 325g can bamboo shoots, drained
1 medium carrot
1 small green cucumber, peeled
100g baby mushrooms
DRESSING
1 tablespoon oil
2 tablespoons sesame oil
¼ cup lemon juice
1 tablespoon sake
2 teaspoons sugar
2 cloves garlic, crushed
¼ cup toasted sesame seeds

Trim and peel asparagus, boil, steam or microwave for about 8 minutes or until just tender; drain, place into bowl of iced water; drain, cut into 5cm pieces. Drop snow peas into pan of boiling water, drain immediately, place into bowl of iced water; drain. Slice lotus root thinly; cut bamboo shoots, carrot and cucumber into 5cm strips, combine with asparagus, snow peas, mushrooms. Toss through Dressing.

Dressing: Combine all the ingredients, mix well.

SNOW WHITE STRAWBERRY JELLY
5g agar-agar strands (about 30 strands) or 2 tablespoons gelatine
1 cup water
1½ cups sugar
2 egg whites
1 teaspoon grated lemon rind
1 tablespoon lemon juice
½ x 250g punnet strawberries

ABOVE: Snow White Strawberry Jelly

Cut agar-agar into 2.5cm strips with scissors, place in pan with water, stand 30 minutes. (If using gelatine, combine gelatine, water and sugar in pan, stir over low heat without boiling until gelatine is completely dissolved, remove from heat, cool to room temperature.)

Stir agar-agar mixture over heat, without boiling, until agar-agar is dissolved — this will take about 10 minutes. Strain mixture through muslin-lined sieve, return to pan, add sugar,

stir over heat, without boiling, until sugar is dissolved, cool to room temperature. Beat egg whites in small basin with electric mixer until firm peaks form, gradually add agar-agar or gelatine mixture in thin stream while mixer is operating. Beat in lemon rind and juice, beat until thick, spread into lightly oiled lamington tin (base measures 16cm × 26cm). Press strawberries into mixture, smooth top, refrigerate several hours or until set.

KOREA

Pickled cabbage (kim chee or kimchi) is prepared each autumn for the rest of the year. There are many variations on this traditional recipe which is usually based on radish or cabbage. It is served at every meal as an accompaniment.

KOREAN DINNER PARTY FOR FOUR

- CRISPY SESAME PRAWNS
- MARINATED BEEF SPARE RIBS
- PICKLED CABBAGE
- MIXED VEGETABLES AND NOODLES
- MUNG BEAN PANCAKES
- PERSIMMON LIME ICE

The food in this dinner party is rich in flavor and the Persimmon Lime Ice dessert complements the meal perfectly. Most of the preparation is done the day before; last minute cooking is kept down to a minimum.

RIGHT: Clockwise from front: Crispy Sesame Prawns, Pickled Cabbage, Marinated Beef Spare Ribs, Mung Bean Pancakes, Mixed Vegetables and Noodles.

Table, screen, black lacquered platters and triangular plate from Chin Hua Galleries, Crows Nest, NSW; china is Malabar by Wedgwood.

CRISPY SESAME PRAWNS

Serve soy sauce as a dipping sauce with prawns.

12 (about 500g) green king prawns
125g minced beef steak
1 green shallot, chopped
1 small clove garlic, crushed
½ teaspoon sesame oil
2 teaspoons sesame seeds
oil for deep frying
BATTER
1 cup cornflour
2 eggs
⅓ cup water
2 tablespoons sesame seeds

STEP 1
Peel prawns leaving tails intact. Using a sharp knife, cut prawns down the back, cutting nearly all the way through; remove vein, flatten prawns slightly.

STEP 2
Combine mince with shallot, garlic, sesame oil and sesame seeds, press evenly over underside of prawns. Dip prawns into Batter, deep fry in hot oil until cooked; drain, serve hot.
Batter: Blend or process cornflour, eggs and water until smooth; stir in sesame seeds.

MARINATED BEEF SPARE RIBS

Use a small mortar and pestle (available from kitchen shops) to crush the sesame seeds thoroughly. Ask butcher to cut spare ribs into 5cm pieces.

2kg beef spare ribs
1 tablespoon sesame seeds
6 green shallots, finely chopped
2 teaspoons grated fresh ginger
2 tablespoons sugar
⅓ cup dark soy sauce
2 cloves garlic, crushed
2 tablespoons dry sherry

Trim fat from ribs, cut deep slits in meat to allow marinade to penetrate. Crush sesame seeds in mortar and pestle (this releases the oil and flavor from the seeds). Place seeds in heavy-based pan, stir constantly over heat until lightly browned.

Combine sesame seeds with shallots, ginger, sugar, soy sauce, garlic and sherry, add ribs, mix well, cover, refrigerate overnight.

Remove ribs from marinade, barbecue or grill, turning often until brown and crisp all over; serve immediately. If desired, serve remaining marinade as a dipping sauce.

BELOW: Persimmon Lime Ice

PICKLED CABBAGE

Pickled Cabbage is served as an accompaniment to main course dishes.

1 Chinese chard
¼ cup cooking salt
1 medium carrot, grated
1 red pepper, finely sliced
2 cloves garlic, crushed
1 teaspoon grated fresh ginger
2 teaspoons sugar
1 teaspoon cooking salt, extra

Place whole cabbage in large bowl, sprinkle with salt, cover, stand several hours. Wash cabbage under cold water, drain well. Combine carrot and pepper with garlic, ginger, sugar and extra salt, mix well.

Cut cabbage in half lengthwise, pack carrot mixture between cabbage leaves, place in a large bowl, cover, refrigerate for 1 to 2 days before using.

MIXED VEGETABLES AND NOODLES

250g vermicelli noodles
2 tablespoons oil
2 cloves garlic, crushed
1 teaspoon ground black pepper
8 green shallots, finely sliced
2 medium carrots, grated
2 medium zucchini, grated
2 tablespoons sesame oil
2 tablespoons light soy sauce

Add noodles to large pan of rapidly boiling water, boil 2 minutes or until just tender; drain, rinse well under cold water; drain.

Heat oil in wok, add garlic, pepper and shallots, stir-fry 1 minute, add carrots, zucchini, stir-fry until just tender. Add noodles, sesame oil and soy sauce, stir through quickly and lightly.

MUNG BEAN PANCAKES

We used mung bean sprouts in this recipe. A large heavy-based pan or electric fry pan is ideal for cooking.

½ cup dried yellow mung beans
½ cup water
2 eggs
1 large bacon rasher, chopped
1 small onion, chopped
1 green shallot, chopped
1 clove garlic, crushed
black pepper
1 teaspoon grated fresh ginger
½ cup bean sprouts
¼ teaspoon sesame oil
½ teaspoon chopped fresh red chilli
¼ cup oil

Wash dried mung beans, place in bowl, cover well with water, stand overnight, rinse, drain well. Place into processor or blender with the ½ cup water and eggs, process until just combined, pour into bowl.

Cook bacon and onion in pan until lightly browned, add to bean mixture with shallot, garlic, black pepper, ginger, bean sprouts, sesame oil and chilli, mix well. Heat oil in pan, add mixture, spread out to edge of pan with spatula, cook until golden brown underneath. Place pan under hot griller to set top slightly; this makes pancake easier to turn. Use two spatulas to turn pancake over; brown pancake on other side until golden brown, cut into wedges.

PERSIMMON LIME ICE

Persimmons used in this dish should be as ripe as possible.

4 large (500g) persimmons, peeled
½ cup sugar
1½ cups water
¼ cup lime juice
2 egg whites

Process or blend persimmons until smooth; strain. Combine sugar and water in pan, stir over heat, without boiling, until sugar is dissolved. Bring to boil, reduce heat, simmer, uncovered, 10 minutes without stirring; cool. Stir in persimmon puree and lime juice, pour into lamington tin, cover, freeze until partly set. Process egg whites and persimmon mixture until smooth, pour back into lamington tin, cover, freeze overnight or until set.

THAILAND

The complexity of its flavors imbues Thai cooking with a special excitement; exotic fruit and vegetables, flavorsome herbs and esoteric spices make this a flamboyant cuisine.

The heat of these dishes can be adjusted simply by increasing or decreasing the chilli. As well as being hot, the food is full of the flavor of fresh herbs and sauces traditional in Thai cooking.

RIGHT: Clockwise from front: Tasty Curry Triangles, Chicken with Mixed Vegetables, Herbed Mussels with Hot Lemon Sauce, Pork, Prawns and Fruit Salad, Spicy Beef Cabbage Rolls.

Painting and fruit stand from Thai Tourist Bureau, Sydney; cutlery from SCT Co. Ltd, Sydney; China is Sandhurst by Noritake; dipping sauce dish in centre from Pailin Restaurant, Sydney.

TASTY CURRY TRIANGLES

Unbaked Triangles can be made several hours ahead of cooking time, or can be frozen for up to one month. Deep fry in frozen state.

1 chicken breast fillet
125g lean beef steak
1 medium potato
1 onion, finely chopped
1 tablespoon oil
1 tablespoon curry powder
2 teaspoons sugar
12 sheets 12cm x 12cm Spring Roll
 Pastry
1 egg, lightly beaten
oil for deep frying

Cut potato into 1cm cubes, cook in boiling water 2 minutes, drain. Mince or process chicken and beef.

Heat oil in wok, add potato, onion, chicken, beef, curry powder and sugar, cook, stirring, until mixture is lightly browned. Reduce heat, cook for about 30 minutes, stirring occasionally, until mixture is thick and pasty. Cool to room temperature. Place teaspoonfuls of filling in centre of each wrapper. Brush around edge with egg. Fold in sides and fold over in half (see picture, left). Deep fry in hot oil for about 2 minutes or until golden brown.

Makes 12.

TASTY CURRY TRIANGLES

CHICKEN WITH MIXED VEGETABLES

HERBED MUSSELS WITH HOT LEMON SAUCE

SPICY BEEF CABBAGE ROLLS

PORK, PRAWNS AND FRUIT SALAD

BANANAS IN COCONUT CREAM

KEY TO PREVIOUS PAGE

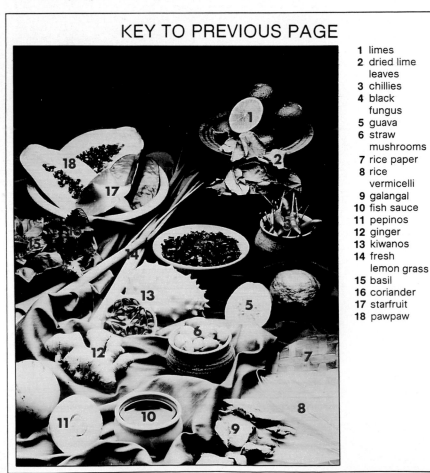

1 limes
2 dried lime leaves
3 chillies
4 black fungus
5 guava
6 straw mushrooms
7 rice paper
8 rice vermicelli
9 galangal
10 fish sauce
11 pepinos
12 ginger
13 kiwanos
14 fresh lemon grass
15 basil
16 coriander
17 starfruit
18 pawpaw

THAI
EXOTICALLY HOT
DINNER PARTY
FOR SIX

CHICKEN WITH MIXED VEGETABLES

Chicken can be marinated several hours ahead of cooking time or refrigerate overnight if desired.

6 chicken breast fillets
1 teaspoon grated fresh ginger
1 tablespoon dry sherry
1 bunch asparagus
1 carrot
2 tablespoons oil
2 cloves garlic, crushed
2 large fresh red chillies, finely chopped
400g can baby corn, drained
425g can straw mushrooms, drained
2 tablespoons water
60g snow peas
1 cup bean sprouts
3 green shallots, chopped
2 teaspoons cornflour
½ cup chicken stock
1 tablespoon fish sauce
½ teaspoon sesame oil

Cut chicken into thin strips. Combine chicken, ginger and dry sherry in bowl, stand 1 hour. Peel asparagus, cut asparagus diagonally into 5cm lengths. Cut carrot into thin strips. Heat oil, garlic and chillies in wok, add chicken, stir-fry 3 minutes; remove from wok. Add asparagus, carrot, corn, mushrooms and water, stir-fry 2 minutes. Add remaining vegetables and chicken, then combined blended cornflour, stock, fish sauce and sesame oil, stir-fry further 2 minutes.

HERBED MUSSELS WITH HOT LEMON SAUCE

1kg mussels
1 cup fresh basil leaves
4 green shallots, chopped
1 cup water
HOT LEMON SAUCE
½ cup lemon juice
¼ cup water
2 tablespoons fish sauce
1 teaspoon sugar
2 cloves garlic, crushed
1 tablespoon chopped fresh coriander
2 small fresh red chillies, finely chopped

Clean mussels, remove beard. Combine basil, shallots and water in large pan, bring to boil, reduce heat, simmer, uncovered, 10 minutes. Add mussels, cover, cook 3 minutes, or until mussels open. Discard any mussels which do not open. Serve mussels with Hot Lemon Sauce.

Hot Lemon Sauce: Combine all the ingredients thoroughly.

SPICY BEEF CABBAGE ROLLS

Beef may be cooked on day of serving.

1kg minced beef steak
1 onion, finely chopped
3 tablespoons chopped fresh mint
2 tablespoons chopped fresh lemon grass
¼ cup fish sauce
1½ tablespoons lemon juice
1 red pepper, finely chopped
2 green shallots, finely chopped
1 tablespoon chopped fresh coriander
4 red cabbage leaves
4 green cabbage leaves

Bring 2 cups of water to the boil in pan, add mince, break up with a fork, return to the boil, cook 1 minute. Drain mince, discard water, cool mince to room temperature (do not refrigerate or fat will set).

Mix onion, mint, lemon grass, fish sauce, lemon juice, pepper, shallots and coriander into mince. Bring large pan of water to the boil, add cabbage leaves, cook 1 minute; drain. Divide mince mixture between cabbage leaves, roll up firmly. Serve rolls at room temperature.

Makes 8.

PORK, PRAWNS AND FRUIT SALAD

If desired, prepare salad, except apples, several hours ahead. Add apple slices and prepared Dressing to salad just before serving.

500g cooked prawns
125g barbecued pork
2 green apples, sliced
2 mangoes, sliced
1 small pineapple, sliced
DRESSING
2 tablespoons lemon juice
1 teaspoon sugar
1 tablespoon fish sauce

Shell prawns, leaving tails intact. Cut pork into thin strips. Arrange apples, mangoes, pineapple, pork and prawns on serving plate, top with Dressing just before serving.

Dressing: Combine all ingredients.

BANANAS IN COCONUT CREAM

6 firm bananas, sliced
415ml can coconut cream
½ cup brown sugar
½ teaspoon jasmine essence
½ cup water

Combine all ingredients in pan, bring to the boil, reduce heat, simmer, uncovered, 3 minutes; serve hot.

ABOVE: From left; Pork, Prawns and Fruit Salad, Herbed Mussels with Hot Lemon Sauce, Spicy Beef Cabbage Rolls. RIGHT: Bananas in Coconut Cream.

THAI
LIGHT AND TASTY
DINNER PARTY
FOR FOUR

SEAFOOD AND LEMON GRASS SOUP

PORK WITH CRISPY NOODLES

MARINATED HERBED QUAIL WITH CARROT SALAD

CHILLI DIPPING SAUCE

BROCCOLI WITH OYSTER SAUCE

MOIST COCONUT PIE

This menu, featuring light, citrus-flavored food, is quick and easy to prepare. The only chilli is in the Dipping Sauce, which should be served throughout the dinner; this way you and your guests have the choice of mild or hot taste sensations. We chose to serve the dessert cold, but it is excellent served hot; let it stand five minutes before cutting into wedges.

SEAFOOD AND LEMON GRASS SOUP

Add seafood to soup just before serving, do not reheat or prawns will become quite tough.

250g white fish fillets, chopped
500g green prawns, shelled
1 litre (4 cups) chicken stock
2 tablespoons finely chopped lemon grass
6 Kaffir lime leaves
3 pieces dried galangal
2 tablespoons lemon juice
2 teaspoons fish sauce
1 tablespoon chopped fresh coriander
340ml can coconut milk

Combine stock, lemon grass, lime leaves and galangal in large pan, bring to the boil, reduce heat, simmer, uncovered, 15 minutes. Add lemon juice, fish sauce, coriander, coconut milk and seafood, cook few minutes, or until prawns turn pink.

PORK WITH CRISPY NOODLES

125g rice vermicelli
oil for deep frying
1 cup (100g) bean sprouts, firmly packed
1 tablespoon chopped fresh coriander
2 green shallots, chopped
LIME SYRUP
½ cup water
½ cup lime juice
½ cup sugar
PORK MIXTURE
500g pork mince
2 tablespoons oil
1 onion, chopped
2 cloves garlic, crushed
2 teaspoons shrimp paste
2 tablespoons tomato paste
⅓ cup fish sauce

Heat oil in wok, add uncooked noodles to oil. They will immediately puff up; turn quickly, cook other side. This should only take a few seconds; drain noodles on absorbent paper. Mix Lime Syrup, Pork Mixture, bean sprouts, coriander, shallots through noodles.

Lime Syrup: Combine water, lime juice and sugar in pan, stir, without boiling, until sugar is dissolved, bring to boil, boil, uncovered, 3 minutes; cool to room temperature.

Pork Mixture: Heat oil in wok, add onion and garlic, stir-fry 1 minute. Add pork and shrimp paste, stir-fry 5 minutes, add tomato paste and fish sauce, stir-fry further 3 minutes.

LEFT: Back, from left: Seafood and Lemon Grass Soup, Pork with Crispy Noodles, Chilli Dipping Sauce; front, from left: Broccoli with Oyster Sauce, Marinated Herbed Quail with Carrot Salad.

China from Sala Thai Restaurant, Sydney.

BROCCOLI WITH OYSTER SAUCE

2 bacon rashers, finely chopped
1kg broccoli
2 tablespoons oil
1 clove garlic, crushed
2 teaspoons oyster sauce
1 tablespoon fish sauce
1 teaspoon bean sauce
2 teaspoons cornflour
¼ cup water

Stir-fry bacon in wok until crisp; drain on absorbent paper. Cut broccoli into small flowerets. Bring pan of water to boil, add broccoli, cook 5 minutes; drain and rinse under cold water; drain.

Heat oil and garlic in wok, add broccoli, stir-fry 1 minute. Blend oyster sauce, fish sauce and bean sauce with cornflour and water, stir into broccoli mixture, stir-fry further 2 minutes, or until mixture boils and thickens; sprinkle with bacon just before serving.

MOIST COCONUT PIE

Pie can be made a day before required.

4 eggs
125g butter, softened
½ cup plain flour
½ cup milk
1 cup castor sugar
1 cup coconut
400ml can coconut milk

Blend or process all ingredients until smooth, pour into greased 23cm pie plate, bake in moderate oven 1 hour. Cool to room temperature, turn onto serving plate. If desired, decorate with whipped cream, glace cherries and toasted shredded coconut.

MARINATED HERBED QUAIL WITH CARROT SALAD

6 quail
2 tablespoons walnut oil
½ cup chopped fresh basil
½ cup chopped fresh coriander
2 teaspoons grated fresh ginger
2 cloves garlic, crushed
2 teaspoons grated lime rind
2 tablespoons lime juice
2 tablespoons light soy sauce
1 tablespoon sugar
CARROT SALAD
2 carrots
1 stick celery
1 tablespoon rice vinegar
3 tablespoons walnut oil
1 tablespoon lemon juice
1 teaspoon sugar
1 tablespoon chopped walnuts

Cut quail in half. Combine remaining ingredients in shallow ovenproof dish, add quail, marinate several hours or overnight in refrigerator. Bake in moderate oven 30 minutes or until quail are golden brown. Serve with Carrot Salad.
Carrot Salad: Cut carrots and celery into thin strips about 5cm in length. Combine vinegar, oil, lemon juice and sugar in bowl, pour over vegetables, sprinkle with walnuts.

CHILLI DIPPING SAUCE

2 tablespoons lemon juice
2 tablespoons fish sauce
2 teaspoons light soy sauce
3 tablespoons sugar
1 small fresh red chilli, finely chopped
1 green shallot, finely chopped

Mix all ingredients together.

ABOVE: Moist Coconut Pie.
BELOW: Back: Chilli Dipping Sauce; front: Marinated Herbed Quail with Carrot Salad.

74

VIETNAM

Lightness and subtlety are the hallmarks of Vietnamese cooking, with flavors delicate but distinct. Simmering is a popular Vietnamese cooking technique; oil is kept to a minimum.

VIETNAMESE
FESTIVE DINNER PARTY FOR SIX

PRAWNS IN GARLIC TOMATO SAUCE

SPRING ROLLS WITH HOT FISH SAUCE AND GREEN SALAD

BEEF AND BEAN SPROUTS WITH NOODLES

PORK WITH LEMON GRASS

CHICKEN AND CRAB SOUP

CARAMEL COCONUT FLANS

Much of the food in this dinner party can be prepared the day before required. The food is light and delicate in flavor. Serve rice and the Hot Fish Sauce throughout the meal and serve the soup just before dessert.

PRAWNS IN GARLIC TOMATO SAUCE
1kg green king prawns, shelled
3 tablespoons oil
3 cloves garlic, crushed
1 tablespoon tomato paste
Devein prawns leaving tails intact. Heat oil in wok, add garlic, stir-fry 30 seconds. Add prawns and tomato paste, stir-fry 3 minutes or until prawns turn pink and are tender.

HOT FISH SAUCE
Hot Fish Sauce is generally served throughout the meal. It can be covered and refrigerated for up to one week.

1 small fresh red chilli, chopped
2 cloves garlic, crushed
2½ tablespoons fish sauce
2 teaspoons lime juice
3 teaspoons sugar
¼ cup water
Combine all ingredients in bowl, stir until sugar is dissolved.
 Makes about ½ cup.

GREEN SALAD
Have guests place a Spring Roll in centre of a lettuce leaf, add a little mint, coriander and cucumber and roll up. Dip rolls into Hot Fish Sauce.

1 lettuce
fresh mint leaves
fresh coriander leaves
1 cucumber, sliced
Arrange all ingredients on serving plate, cover, refrigerate until needed.

BELOW: Clockwise from Back: Chicken and Crab Soup, Prawns in Garlic Tomato Sauce; Spring Rolls with Hot Fish Sauce and Green Salad.

China is Intrigue, Vogue Collection by Royal Doulton.

SPRING ROLLS

We used Thai rice paper, 16cm in diameter, for this recipe, but Spring Roll Wrappers could be substituted. Rolls should be prepared no more than several hours ahead of cooking, covered and refrigerated. They can be frozen, uncooked, for up to two months.

18 dried rice paper wrappers
1 egg, lightly beaten
1 tablespoon water
oil for deep frying
FILLING
500g pork mince
2 teaspoons black fungus
½ x 230g can water chestnuts, drained, chopped
1 small onion, finely chopped
1 clove garlic, crushed
1 carrot, grated
½ x 185g can crab, drained
2 teaspoons cornflour
½ teaspoon sesame oil
1 egg, lightly beaten

Brush combined egg and water over rice paper, stand several minutes to soften. Place tablespoonfuls of Filling evenly on short end of each rectangle, fold in sides and roll up. Deep fry rolls in hot oil for about 3 minutes, or until golden brown and cooked through; drain. Do not have oil too hot or rolls will brown before they are cooked through. Serve with Hot Fish Sauce and Green Salad.

Filling: Cover fungus with cold water, stand 30 minutes, rinse; drain, chop finely. Combine pork mince, water chestnuts, onion, garlic, carrot, crab, cornflour, sesame oil and egg, beat with wooden spoon until well mixed.

BEEF AND BEAN SPROUTS WITH NOODLES

1kg rump steak
500g rice vermicelli
2 tablespoons oil
2 onions, chopped
1 clove garlic, crushed
1 red pepper, chopped
1 tablespoon fish sauce
½ cup roasted unsalted peanuts, chopped
1 lettuce
1 cup (100g) bean sprouts, firmly packed

Add vermicelli to large pan of boiling water, boil for 5 minutes while steak is cooking; drain well. Trim excess fat from steak, cut steak into thin strips. Heat oil in wok, add steak, onions, garlic and pepper, stir-fry until steak is tender. Add fish sauce, stir-fry 1 minute. Sprinkle peanuts over steak, serve with noodles, lettuce, bean sprouts.

PORK WITH LEMON GRASS

5 pork loin chops
2 teaspoons oil
1 onion
1 stem lemon grass, finely chopped
2 green shallots, finely chopped
3 tablespoons oil, extra
1 tablespoon fish sauce
1½ teaspoons sugar
1½ teaspoons sambal oelek
1 teaspoon cornflour
1 tablespoon water
1 tablespoon unsalted roasted peanuts, chopped

Remove rind and excess fat from chops, slice pork thinly, combine with oil. Cut onion in half, then into thin wedges. Place shallots in bowl. Heat extra oil in wok, spoon 1 tablespoon of the hot oil over shallots in bowl. Add onion to remaining oil in wok, stir-fry 1 minute. Add pork, stir-fry until pork is tender. Add lemon grass, fish sauce, sugar, sambal oelek, blended cornflour and water. Stir-fry over high heat until mixture boils and thickens. Spoon pork mixture onto plate, top with shallot mixture, sprinkle with peanuts.

CARAMEL COCONUT FLANS

If desired, make flans the day before required; keep covered in refrigerator.

SYRUP
¾ cup sugar
¾ cup water
CUSTARD
340ml can coconut cream
½ cup milk
½ cup sugar
4 eggs

Syrup: Combine sugar and water in pan, stir over heat, without boiling, until sugar is dissolved. Bring to the boil, boil rapidly without stirring for about 5 minutes, or until mixture turns golden brown. Pour mixture into 6 small flan dishes, rotate dishes so that caramel coats base of dishes evenly.

Custard: Whisk coconut cream, milk, sugar and eggs together in bowl. Strain mixture into flan dishes. Bring water to boil in large pan, place flans in steamer or over rack in pan, cover, steam for 20 minutes or until Custard is just set. Remove from pan; cool to room temperature before refrigerating. Turn onto plates just before serving.

CHICKEN AND CRAB SOUP

Stock for soup can be made up to two days before serving.

250g pork mince
2 green shallots, finely chopped
1 egg yolk
1 teaspoon tomato paste
1 teaspoon fish sauce
185g can crab, drained
2 litres (8 cups) chicken stock
½ cup tapioca or sago
1 tablespoon fish sauce, extra
2 teaspoons light soy sauce
**2 tablespoons chopped fresh
  coriander**
2 green shallots, chopped, extra

Combine pork, shallots, egg yolk, tomato paste, fish sauce and crab in bowl, mix well. Roll teaspoonfuls of mixture into balls. Bring stock to boil in pan, add balls, reboil, reduce heat, simmer, uncovered, 10 minutes. Soak tapioca in cold water 5 minutes; drain. Stir tapioca into soup, bring to boil, cook 2 minutes. Add extra fish sauce, soy sauce, coriander and extra shallots.

ABOVE: From left: Pork with Lemon Grass, Beef and Bean Sprouts with Noodles.
RIGHT: Caramel Coconut Flans.

VIETNAMESE CASUAL HOT POT DINNER PARTY FOR SIX

SEAFOOD HOT POT

DELICIOUS STUFFED
CHICKEN WINGS

FLUFFY BANANA
COCONUT DESSERTS

A hot pot dinner party is an informal, friendly way to entertain. The hot pots are inexpensive and readily available from Asian food stores; you also need the small wire baskets in which to cook the food. If preferred, the stock can be made, then seafood and vegetables added and served as a delicious main course soup in individual bowls. Or the stock can be made in an electric frying pan.

SEAFOOD HOT POT

Supply each guest with a small wire basket in which to cook the seafood.

To prepare the Hot Pot: Use heat beads available for use in barbecues. Set the beads alight and burn them until white hot — the best way to do this is in a barbecue or hibachi. While the heat beads are burning, stand the hot pot on a thick piece of solid wood to protect the surface on which the pot stands. Using tongs, quickly place the white hot beads down the chimney of the hot pot; then pour the boiling stock into the hot pot.

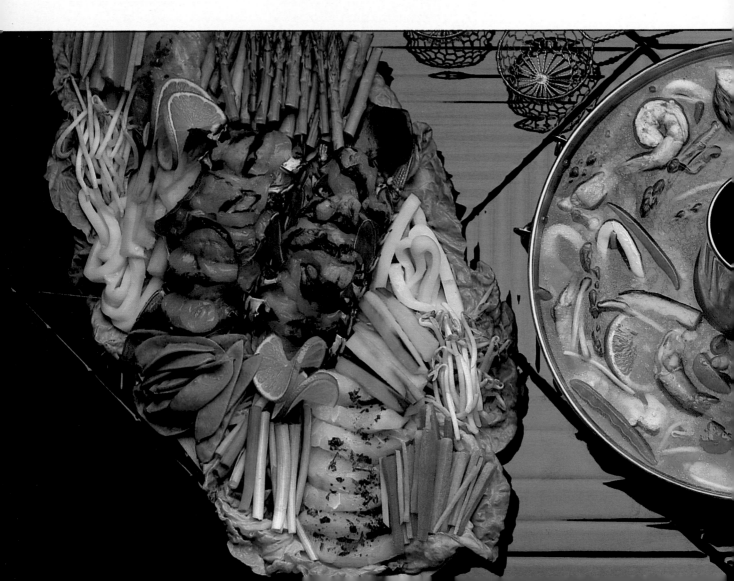

2 green lobster tails
500g white fish fillets, chopped
1kg green king prawns, shelled
500g squid
2 tablespoons sesame oil
¼ cup lemon juice
1 large fresh red chilli, finely
    chopped
2 cloves garlic, crushed
2 tablespoons chopped coriander
2 tablespoons ground black pepper
1 lettuce
2 cucumbers, peeled, seeded
6 green shallots
2 medium carrots
5cm piece fresh green ginger, peeled
250g bunch fresh asparagus
200g snow peas
2½ cups (250g) bean sprouts, firmly
    packed
FISH STOCK
1 large snapper head
2 litres (8 cups) water
3 green shallots, chopped
5cm piece fresh green ginger, peeled
1 teaspoon whole black peppercorns
2 chicken stock cubes
2 tablespoons fish sauce
2 tablespoons sesame oil
1 lime, sliced

Remove lobster from shell, cut lobster into 2cm slices, mix with sesame oil. Combine cleaned squid with lemon juice; combine prawns with chilli and garlic. Combine fish with coriander and black pepper. Cover all seafood, refrigerate several hours.

Separate, wash and drain lettuce. Cut cucumbers and shallots into 5cm strips. Cut carrots and ginger into fine 5cm strips and combine. Peel and trim asparagus, cut into 5cm pieces. Top and tail snow peas, trim bean sprouts. Arrange all vegetables and seafood on platter. Place simmering Fish Stock into the hot pot.

Fish Stock: Combine fish head, water, shallots, chopped ginger and peppercorns in pan, bring to boil, reduce heat, cover, simmer 2 hours, cool, strain through fine sieve. Add crumbled stock cubes, fish sauce, sesame oil and lime before reheating.

BELOW: From left: A selection of fresh seafood and vegetables, Seafood Hot Pot, Delicious Stuffed Chicken Wings.

China is Blue Siam by Wedgwood; Tiles from Fred Pazotti Pty. Ltd., Woollahra, NSW.

DELICIOUS STUFFED CHICKEN WINGS

We used the 'Lungkow' brand of vermicelli noodles for this recipe.

1½kg chicken wings
8 dried mushrooms
100g packet vermicelli bean
    noodles (cellophane noodles)
1 teaspoon sesame oil
1 tablespoon hoisin sauce
1 cup Chinese shredded cabbage
1 cup grated carrot
1 small red pepper, finely sliced
1 tablespoon grated fresh ginger
oil for deep frying
1 tablespoon hoisin sauce, extra
1 tablespoon rice vinegar
1 tablespoon honey

STEP 1
Without cutting through skin, cut chicken flesh away from bones down to the first joint.

STEP 2
Pull flesh back over joint, remove bone at joint. Cut flesh away from joint to expose two smaller bones.

STEP 3
Pull flesh back over two smaller bones and remove bones at next joint with knife, return chicken wing to normal shape ready for filling.

STEP 4
Place mushrooms in bowl, cover with boiling water, cover, stand 20 minutes, remove and discard stalks, chop mushrooms into thin strips. Cook vermicelli noodles in pan of boiling water 5 minutes; drain, chop roughly, return to pan, add sesame oil and hoisin sauce, mix well. Add mushrooms, cabbage, carrot, red pepper and ginger, mix well. Place filling into boned chicken wings; secure openings with toothpicks. Deep fry in hot oil until golden brown; drain on absorbent paper, serve with combined extra hoisin sauce, rice vinegar and honey as a dipping sauce.

BELOW: Fluffy Banana Coconut Desserts.

FLUFFY BANANA COCONUT DESSERTS

These desserts are light, similar to a souffle; serve immediately after baking.

1 cup roughly mashed bananas
(about 2 large ripe bananas)
415ml can coconut cream
6 eggs, separated
30g butter, melted
½ cup cream
¼ cup brown sugar
2 tablespoons plain flour
2 teaspoons grated orange rind
1 tablespoon orange juice

Blend or process bananas and coconut cream, until smooth. Add egg yolks, butter, cream, sugar, flour, orange rind and juice, blend 10 seconds, transfer to large bowl. Beat egg whites in small bowl with electric mixer until soft peaks form, fold lightly through banana mixture. Spoon into 6 individual dishes (1 cup capacity), place on oven tray, bake in moderate oven for about 20 minutes or until puffy. Serve with whipped cream.

Many specialist ingredients are used in Malaysian cuisine; coconut flesh and milk are essential to many recipes and noodles are widely used.

KEY TO PREVIOUS PAGE

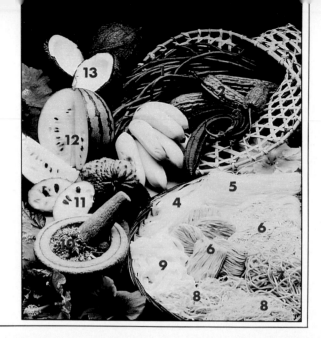

1 snake beans
2 bitter melon
3 Chinese gourd
4 dried rice sticks
5 dried rice vermicelli
6 dried egg noodles
7 hokkien noodles
8 fresh egg noodles
9 fresh rice noodles
10 mixed spices
11 custard apples
12 yellow melon
13 coconuts

LAMB AND POTATO IN LETTUCE CUPS

CHICKEN WITH COCONUT CURRY SAUCE

SQUID WITH BLACK BEAN SAUCE

CHILLI FRIED RICE NOODLES

GREEN SALAD WITH LEMON CREAM DRESSING

MIXED MELON AND GINGER FRUIT SALAD

MALAYSIAN PIQUANT DINNER PARTY FOR SIX

Most of the preparation and some of the cooking can be done the day before the dinner party. Serve the Lamb and Potato in Lettuce Cups as an entree then the remaining savory dishes all together if possible. The Melon and Ginger Fruit Salad — served well chilled, topped with the delicious, delicately-flavored coconut cream — is a fitting end to this zesty-tasting dinner party.

LAMB AND POTATO IN LETTUCE CUPS

This dish can be cooked up to the stage of stirring in the cooked potato, the day before required. Reheat and add potato when ready to serve.

4 lamb forequarter chops
6 large lettuce leaves
30g (about 8) dried mushrooms
1 large potato
¾ cup oil
1 large onion, chopped
1 small red pepper, chopped
1 clove garlic, crushed
1 teaspoon grated fresh ginger
2 teaspoons cornflour
½ cup water
1 teaspoon sesame oil
2 teaspoons soy sauce
1 tablespoon hoisin sauce

Trim lettuce cups to an even size with scissors. Cover mushrooms with boiling water, stand 20 minutes; drain, remove and discard stems, chop caps roughly. Cut potato and lamb into small cubes. Heat oil in wok, add potato, fry until golden brown and just tender, remove from wok; drain. Reserve 1 tablespoon of the oil in wok, reheat oil, add lamb, stir-fry over high heat until lamb is well browned all over. Add onion, pepper, garlic and ginger, stir-fry until onion is soft, add mushrooms, stir-fry 1 minute. Blend cornflour with water, add sesame oil and sauces, add to wok, stir constantly over heat until mixture boils and thickens. Reduce heat, simmer 5 minutes, stir in potatoes, cook until heated through, spoon into lettuce cups to serve.

LEFT: Clockwise from front: Green Salad with Lemon Cream Dressing, Lamb and Potato in Lettuce Cups, Chilli Fried Rice Noodles.

China from Lifestyle Imports, Sydney. Previous page: Hibiscus flowers from Hibiscus Park Nursery, Warriewood, NSW.

CHICKEN WITH COCONUT CURRY SAUCE

Curry Sauce can be made the day before required; cover, refrigerate, reheat in pan or microwave when ready to serve.

6 chicken breast fillets
60g ghee
COCONUT CURRY SAUCE
30g ghee
2 onions, chopped
1 clove garlic, crushed
1 stem lemon grass, chopped
2 small fresh red chillies, finely chopped
¼ teaspoon cinnamon
½ teaspoon cardamom
2 teaspoons curry powder
340ml can coconut milk

Melt ghee in pan, add chicken, fry gently until golden brown and tender; drain, slice. Serve topped with Coconut Curry Sauce.

Coconut Curry Sauce: Melt ghee in pan, add onions, garlic and lemon grass, saute until onions are soft. Add chillies, cinnamon, cardamom and curry, cook, stirring, 1 minute. Stir in coconut milk, simmer, uncovered, 5 minutes. Remove from heat, blend or process until smooth, strain, reheat.

SQUID WITH BLACK BEAN SAUCE

500g squid
200g snow peas
2 red peppers
2 tablespoons oil
1 clove garlic, crushed
1 tablespoon black beans, mashed
3 teaspoons plain flour
1 tablespoon sate sauce
2 teaspoons sesame oil
1 teaspoon sambal oelek
¼ cup water

Cut cleaned squid into rings. Trim snow peas, slice peppers diagonally. Heat oil in wok, add garlic and black beans, stir-fry 1 minute. Add squid, snow peas and peppers, stir-fry few minutes or until squid is tender. Blend flour with sate sauce, sesame oil, sambal oelek and water. Add to wok, stir-fry until mixture boils and thickens.

CHILLI FRIED RICE NOODLES

1kg fresh rice noodles
2 tablespoons oil
2 onions, sliced
125g bacon, chopped
4 small fresh red chillies, finely chopped
2 tablespoons dry sherry
2 cloves garlic, crushed
2 cups (200g) bean sprouts, firmly packed
2 sticks celery, chopped
4 green shallots, chopped
1 tablespoon oil, extra
2 tablespoons light soy sauce
2 tablespoons dark soy sauce

Cut noodles into thin strips. Heat oil in wok, add onions and bacon, stir-fry until onions are lightly browned. Add chilli, sherry and garlic, stir-fry 30 seconds. Add bean sprouts, celery and shallots, stir-fry until vegetables are just tender, remove from wok.

Heat extra oil in wok, add noodles, stir gently until heated through, add soy sauces and vegetable mixture, stir-fry until heated through.

GREEN SALAD WITH LEMON CREAM DRESSING

1 bunch snake beans
2 small green cucumbers
2 green peppers
2 small onions
6 green shallots , sliced
2 tablespoons oil
2 cloves garlic, crushed
1 cup shredded coconut
LEMON CREAM DRESSING
½ cup canned coconut cream
¼ cup lemon juice
2 tablespoons chopped fresh mint

Trim snake beans to 5cm lengths. Peel, seed and cut cucumbers to 5cm lengths, cut peppers, onions and shallots into 5cm lengths.

Heat oil in wok, add garlic and vegetables, stir-fry 1 minute, cool to room temperature. Place coconut on serving plate, top with vegetables, then Lemon Cream Dressing.

Lemon Cream Dressing: Combine all ingredients.

BELOW: From left: Chicken with Coconut Curry Sauce, Green Salad with Lemon Cream Dressing, Squid with Black Bean Sauce.
RIGHT: Mixed Melon and Ginger Fruit Salad.

Mixed Melon and Ginger Fruit Salad glass bowls are Liner from Dansab, Sydney.

MIXED MELON AND GINGER FRUIT SALAD

We used ginger preserved in a syrup for this recipe. This is obtainable in jars at supermarkets and health food stores. The ginger syrup specified in the recipe is from the jar.

1 rockmelon
1 honeydew melon
½ small watermelon
2 tablespoons finely chopped ginger
2 tablespoons ginger syrup
300ml carton thickened cream
1 tablespoon Malibu Coconut
   Liqueur
2 tablespoons brown sugar

Cut rockmelon and honeydew melon in half, remove seeds; remove seeds from watermelon. Make melon balls using melon baller. Combine melon balls in large bowl with ginger and syrup, add any juice from shells of melon. Refrigerate melon mixture 30 minutes. Whip the combined cream, liqueur and sifted brown sugar until firm peaks form, serve with melons.

MALAYSIAN EXOTICALLY SPICY DINNER PARTY FOR SIX

FIERY RICE NOODLE SOUP

BEEF WITH HOT SATAY SAUCE

CHILLI SWEET LOBSTER

COMPRESSED GINGER RICE

STIR-FRIED VEGETABLES WITH PEANUTS

COCONUT CREPES WITH ORANGE SAUCE

BELOW: Back, from left: Chilli Sweet Lobster, Beef with Hot Satay Sauce; front, from left: Fiery Rice Noodle Soup, Stir-Fried Vegetables with Peanuts, Compressed Ginger Rice.

Flowers, leaves from The Flower Man, Double Bay, NSW; China is Florida by Wedgwood. Tiles by Fred Pazotti Pty. Ltd., Woollahra, NSW.

FIERY RICE NOODLE SOUP
100g fresh rice noodles
2 tablespoons oil
2 onions, chopped
2 cloves garlic, crushed
2 stems lemon grass, finely chopped
2 teaspoons curry powder
2 small fresh red chillies, finely chopped
340ml can coconut cream
4 cups (1 litre) chicken stock
375g medium cooked prawns, shelled
1 cup chopped cos lettuce

Add noodles to large pan of boiling water, boil, uncovered, for about 3 minutes or until tender; drain. Rinse noodles under cold water; drain. Place noodles in serving dishes. Heat oil in pan, add onions, garlic and lemon grass, stir-fry until onions are just tender. Stir in curry powder and chillies, stir-fry 1 minute. Add coconut cream, stock, prawns and lettuce, bring to boil, pour over noodles.

STIR-FRIED VEGETABLES WITH PEANUTS
125g roasted unsalted peanuts
1 bunch (about 8) spring onions
1 cucumber, peeled, seeded
125g green beans
2 tablespoons oil
2 carrots, sliced
2 teaspoons turmeric
2 cloves garlic, crushed
8 green shallots, chopped
2 tablespoons white vinegar
2 tablespoons sugar
1 mango, sliced
¾ cup chicken stock

Process peanuts until roughly chopped. Trim and peel onions, cut in half if large. Slice cucumber, cut beans into 2.5cm pieces.

Heat oil in wok, add onions and carrots, stir-fry until lightly browned, add turmeric, garlic, shallots, vinegar and sugar, stir-fry 1 minute. Add mango, cucumber, beans, peanuts and chicken stock, stir-fry 5 minutes or until vegetables are just tender.

Malaysian food is well known to be hot, spicy and tantalising in flavor. Most of the recipes in this menu require last minute cooking, however the Beef Satay and Compressed Rice is better if prepared the day before. Serve the soup first, then the satay, followed by the remaining three savory dishes.

COMPRESSED GINGER RICE

This rice dish can be made the day before required if desired.

2 cups short grain rice
4 cups (1 litre) chicken stock
1 tablespoon grated fresh ginger
Place rice, stock and ginger in pan with tight-fitting lid, bring to boil, reduce heat, simmer, covered, for about 30 minutes or until stock is absorbed and rice is tender. Spoon rice into lamington tin (base measures 16cm X 26cm), cover with a greased piece of foil, cover with a heavy weight such as a book and a few heavy cans of food, or a brick, stand several hours or overnight. Cut rice into 5cm squares with a wet knife. Place onto heatproof serving dish, cover, reheat in moderate oven 15 minutes.

CHILLI SWEET LOBSTER

3 green lobster tails
2 teaspoons grated fresh ginger
1 tablespoon chilli sauce
2 cloves garlic, crushed
1 tablespoon brown sugar
2 tablespoons tomato sauce
1 cup canned tomato puree
½ cup water
2 tablespoons oil
1 cucumber, peeled, seeded
1 red pepper, sliced
Remove lobster flesh from shells, chop flesh roughly. Combine ginger, chilli sauce, garlic, brown sugar, tomato sauce, tomato puree and water in pan, bring to the boil, reduce heat, simmer, uncovered, 5 minutes.

Slice cucumber finely. Heat oil in wok, add lobster, cucumber and pepper, stir-fry until lobster is just tender, add chilli sauce mixture, stir-fry until heated through.

BEEF WITH HOT SATAY SAUCE

1kg rump steak (in one piece)
½ cup brown sugar
2 cloves garlic, crushed
1 tablespoon cumin seeds
1 tablespoon fennel seeds
1 tablespoon coriander seeds
1 small fresh red chilli, finely
   chopped
½ cup finely chopped almonds
½ cup finely chopped roasted
   unsalted peanuts
HOT SATAY SAUCE
¾ cup (150g) roasted unsalted
   peanuts
2 tablespoons oil
1 stem lemon grass, finely chopped
3 teaspoons sambal oelek
⅓ cup brown sugar
1 tablespoon tamarind sauce
½ cup peanut butter
½ cup water

Trim fat from steak, cut steak into 5cm strips, mix well with brown sugar, garlic, seeds, chilli and nuts, cover, marinate several hours or overnight. Thread steak onto skewers, grill or barbecue until tender. Serve with Hot Satay Sauce.

Hot Satay Sauce: Heat oil in pan, add peanuts, lemon grass and sambal oelek, stir-fry 1 minute, add brown sugar, tamarind sauce, peanut butter and water, reduce heat, simmer, stirring for about 3 minutes.

COCONUT CREPES WITH ORANGE SAUCE

Crepes can be made the day before required, covered and refrigerated.

CREPES
4 eggs
¼ cup water
2 tablespoons castor sugar
1 cup plain flour
340g can coconut milk
COCONUT FILLING
90g butter
½ cup castor sugar
1 egg
2 teaspoons grated orange rind
1 tablespoon orange juice
1 cup coconut
ORANGE SAUCE
2 oranges
1 tablespoon cornflour
2 tablespoons sugar
1 cup orange juice
⅓ cup cointreau

Crepes: Blend or process eggs, water, sugar, flour and coconut milk until smooth. Heat a small pan, grease lightly, pour in 2 to 3 tablespoons of mixture. Cook until golden brown. Turn Crepe over, lightly brown other side. Repeat with remaining batter. Makes about 12 Crepes.

Spread Crepes with Coconut Filling, fold Crepes in half then into quarters. Place Crepes into greased ovenproof dish in single layer, cover, bake in moderate oven 10 minutes or until heated through. Serve with hot Sauce.

Coconut Filling: Cream butter and sugar in small bowl with electric mixer until light and fluffy. Add egg, beat well. Stir in orange rind, orange juice and coconut; mix well.

Orange Sauce: Segment oranges. Blend cornflour and sugar in pan with orange juice, stir over heat until mixture boils and thickens (or microwave on HIGH 3 minutes). Stir in cointreau and orange segments.

ABOVE: Coconut Crepes with Orange Sauce

Plate is Xenia by Villeroy & Boch.

INDONESIA

Indonesian cooking, a meld of cultural influences including China, Holland, India and Islam, offers provincial specialities. It can deliver a chilli-hot bite or woo the taste buds with subtler spices.

BELOW: Clockwise from front: Green Bean and Sprout Salad, Hot Potato Curry, Mild Chicken Curry with Tamarind Sauce, Beef Rendang, Mixed Vegetable Pickle, Pineapple Relish.

INDONESIAN RICE TABLE FOR EIGHT

The Rice Table (Rijst-tafel), shown on previous page, is typical of the style of food served in Indonesia. A variety of small side dishes always accompany at least two main courses and rice is served throughout the meal. Both the curries in this menu can be made a day or two ahead of time — in fact the flavor will improve this way. Sweets are generally served between meals in Indonesia, but traditionally, we tend to finish a meal with a dessert.

BEEF RENDANG

May be made a day before required. Keep covered in refrigerator.

1kg rump steak
2 onions, chopped
4 cloves garlic, crushed
3 small fresh red chillies, chopped
1 teaspoon turmeric
2 tablespoons grated fresh ginger
1 tablespoon paprika
⅓ cup water
2 x 400ml cans coconut milk
1 tablespoon finely chopped lemon
   grass
4 Kaffir lime leaves

Combine onions, garlic, chillies, turmeric, ginger, paprika and water in processor, process until smooth and pasty, divide mixture in half.

Cut steak into 2cm cubes, mix well with half the onion mixture. Combine remaining half of the onion mixture with coconut milk, lemon grass and lime leaves in pan, bring to boil, reduce heat, simmer, uncovered, for about 40 minutes or until reduced to about half. Add steak mixture, bring to the boil, reduce heat, simmer, uncovered, for about 1 hour or until steak is tender. Remove lime leaves before serving.

RIGHT: From left: Mixed Vegetable Pickle, Beef Rendang, Pineapple Relish.

PREVIOUS PAGE: Batik fabric is from Java Bazaar, Paddington, NSW; bowls, baskets and dishes from Gallery Nomad, Paddington, NSW.

BEEF RENDANG
MIXED VEGETABLE PICKLE
PINEAPPLE RELISH
MILD CHICKEN CURRY WITH TAMARIND SAUCE
GREEN BEAN AND SPROUT SALAD
HOT POTATO CURRY
MARBLED SPICE CAKE

MIXED VEGETABLE PICKLE

Vegetable Pickle can be served hot or it can be cooled, covered, then refrigerated for up to three days before being served cold.

4 medium onions
2 medium carrots
500g broccoli
6 whole baby chillies
2 cloves garlic, crushed
3 cups chicken stock
¼ cup white vinegar
2 teaspoons sugar
¼ teaspoon turmeric

Cut onions into eighths, cut carrots into 6cm long thin strips. Cut broccoli into small flowerets. Combine all ingredients in pan, bring to the boil, reduce heat, simmer, uncovered, for about 5 minutes or until vegetables are just tender.

PINEAPPLE RELISH

This Relish will keep covered and refrigerated for up to one week.

1 tablespoon oil
1 onion, chopped
2 small fresh red chillies, sliced
¼ teaspoon ground ginger
¼ teaspoon nutmeg
¼ cup sugar
1 pineapple, chopped

Heat oil in pan, add onion and chillies, cook, stirring few minutes. Add ginger, nutmeg, sugar and pineapple, cook, stirring occasionally, for 10 minutes. Cool, place into jar, cover, refrigerate.

MILD CHICKEN CURRY WITH TAMARIND SAUCE

Curry can be made a day or two before required. Keep covered in refrigerator.

2 x No. 15 chickens
½ cup macadamia nuts
4 onions, chopped
1 tablespoon grated fresh ginger
2 cloves garlic, crushed
2 tablespoons oil
1 tablespoon chopped fresh coriander
2 teaspoons ground cumin
1 tablespoon finely chopped lemon grass
2 tablespoons oil, extra
340ml can coconut milk
1 tablespoon cornflour
1 cup chicken stock
2 tablespoons tamarind sauce

Cut chickens into chunky pieces. Combine nuts, onions, ginger and garlic in processor, process until smooth and pasty.

Heat oil in pan, add "paste", coriander, cumin and lemon grass, cook several minutes, stirring constantly until mixture is lightly browned, transfer to deep pan or ovenproof dish.

Heat extra oil in large pan, add chicken in single layer, cook in batches, if necessary, until well browned all over. Add chicken to pan or dish. Stir in coconut milk, blended cornflour and stock and tamarind sauce. Stir constantly over heat until mixture boils and thickens, cover, reduce heat, simmer 45 minutes or until chicken is tender. Or bake, covered, in moderate oven for about 1 hour or until chicken is tender. Serve with rice.

GREEN BEAN AND SPROUT SALAD
500g green beans
2 tablespoons oil
2 tablespoons dried onion flakes
4 hard-boiled eggs
2 cups (200g) bean sprouts
DRESSING
1 clove garlic, crushed
1 teaspoon sugar
2 tablespoons lemon juice
3 tablespoons oil

Top and tail beans; boil, steam or microwave until just tender, rinse under cold water; drain. Heat oil in large pan or wok, add onion flakes, stir constantly over high heat until flakes are lightly browned. This will take about 1 minute. Halve eggs, remove yolks, chop whites roughly. Combine beans and sprouts with Dressing, mix well. Serve beans surrounded by egg whites, sprinkled with egg yolks. Sprinkle beans with fried onions.
Dressing: Combine all ingredients in screw top jar, shake well.

LEFT: Back: Hot Potato Curry; right: Green Bean and Sprout Salad; front: Mild Chicken Curry with Tamarind Sauce.

HOT POTATO CURRY

Make this curry as close to serving time as possible. It is sometimes difficult to reheat potatoes without them breaking up.

1kg potatoes, cubed
60g ghee
6 onions, sliced
3 small fresh red chillies, finely chopped
1 tablespoon curry powder
2 cups chicken stock
1 tablespoon tamarind sauce

Heat ghee in large pan, add potatoes, onions and chillies, cook, stirring constantly for 3 minutes, stir in curry powder, stock and tamarind sauce. Bring to the boil, reduce heat, simmer, uncovered for about 20 minutes or until potatoes are tender.

MARBLED SPICE CAKE

Make cake up to one day ahead if preferred. Or, it can be frozen for up to two months.

250g butter
1½ cups castor sugar
4 eggs
2¼ cups self-raising flour
1 teaspoon mixed spice
1 cup milk
2 tablespoons cocoa
2 tablespoons hot water
pink food coloring
2 teaspoons vanilla

Cream butter and sugar in large bowl with electric mixer until light and fluffy. Add eggs one at a time, beat well after each addition. Add sifted flour and spice alternately with milk, beat on medium speed for 3 minutes or until mixture is smooth. Divide mixture into 3 equal portions, stir in blended cocoa and hot water to one third, pink coloring to one third and vanilla to remaining third. Drop spoonfuls of mixtures, in alternate colors, into greased and base lined deep 23cm round tin. Run a skewer through the mixture several times to give a marbled effect. Bake in moderate oven for about 1 hour, stand few minutes before turning onto wire rack to cool.

The pretty wavy effect on this cake was achieved by cutting wavy strips of paper about 3cm wide and sifting icing sugar into alternating spaces on the top of the cake. We used white icing sugar, combined sifted cocoa and icing sugar, and pink icing sugar. To color icing sugar, simply rub a few drops of pink food coloring into the icing sugar. This is easy if the icing sugar is in a plastic bag with the coloring, work the color through by rubbing the icing sugar through the plastic.

BELOW: Marbled Spice Cake.

INDONESIAN DO-AHEAD LUNCH FOR 10

SPICY MIXED SATES

CORN PUFFS WITH
TOMATO SAUCE

NASI GORENG

GADO GADO

BANANA CITRUS CAKE
WITH ORANGE SYRUP

SPICED PEANUT BISCUITS

All the food in this menu can be prepared in advance. It's a tasty and substantial lunch for 10 people but the recipes can be easily adapted to suit outdoor picnics or barbecues.

SPICY MIXED SATES

Meats can be marinated in Sate Sauce in the refrigerator for up to two days before cooking. If using wooden skewers, soak them in water overnight before using; you will need 30 skewers.

1kg green king prawns
500g rump steak
6 large chicken breast fillets
SATE SAUCE
½ cup roasted salted peanuts
1 onion, chopped
½ cup smooth peanut butter
2 cloves garlic, crushed
⅓ cup chutney
½ cup oil
2 teaspoons light soy sauce
¼ cup lemon juice
½ teaspoon chilli powder

Peel and devein prawns, leaving tails intact. Slice steak into thin strips. Cut chicken into cubes. Thread meat onto skewers; do not combine different meats on the same skewer as they have different cooking times. Brush well with Sate Sauce, grill or barbecue sates until tender, brush occasionally with Sauce during the cooking time.
Sate Sauce: Blend or process peanuts until finely crushed, add onion, process 20 seconds. Add peanut butter, garlic, chutney, oil, soy sauce, lemon juice and chilli, process until smooth.

CORN PUFFS WITH TOMATO SAUCE

Corn mixture can be made the day before required, refrigerate; cook just before serving. Tomato Sauce can be made up to two days ahead, store in refrigerator. Reheat before serving.

3 cobs fresh corn
6 large (1kg) potatoes
¼ cup fruit chutney
⅓ cup plain yoghurt
1 large red pepper, chopped
6 green shallots, chopped
2 cloves garlic, crushed
3 teaspoons curry powder
1½ teaspoons ground cumin
2 eggs, lightly beaten
plain flour
oil for deep frying
TOMATO SAUCE
1 tablespoon oil
2 onions, chopped
pinch chilli powder
2 tablespoons brown sugar
2 x 400g cans tomatoes
2 tablespoons lime juice

Boil, steam or microwave corn; drain, cool. Cut kernels from corn. Boil, steam or microwave potatoes until tender; drain, mash with chutney and yoghurt until smooth (do not use processor). Stir in corn, pepper, shallots, garlic, curry, cumin and eggs. Roll teaspoonfuls of mixture in flour, drop into hot oil, deep fry until golden brown (cook about 6 at a time); drain, serve hot with Sauce.

Tomato Sauce: Heat oil in pan, add onions, cook, stirring, until soft. Add chilli and sugar, cook 1 minute, stir in undrained mashed tomatoes and lime juice. Bring to the boil, reduce heat, simmer, uncovered, about 5 minutes or until tomatoes have softened completely. Blend or process Sauce until smooth, strain, reheat in pan or microwave on HIGH about 3 minutes when ready to serve.

RIGHT: Back, from left: Gado Gado, Corn Puffs with Tomato Sauce; front, from left: Nasi Goreng, Spicy Mixed Sates.

Background fabric, sate platter and basket from Gallery Nomad, Paddington, NSW.

BANANA CITRUS CAKE WITH ORANGE SYRUP

It is essential to use over-ripe bananas for this recipe.

185g butter
1 cup castor sugar
4 eggs
2 cups self-raising flour
½ teaspoon bicarbonate of soda
3 medium bananas
2 tablespoons lemon juice
¼ cup orange juice
ORANGE SYRUP
½ cup sugar
¼ cup water
¼ cup strained orange juice

Cream butter and sugar in small bowl with electric mixer until light and fluffy. Add eggs one at a time, beating well after each addition. Process or blend bananas, lemon and orange juices until smooth and liquefied. Stir sifted flour and soda and banana mixture into creamed mixture. Pour into well greased and lightly floured 20cm baba or ring tin, bake in moderate oven for about 40 minutes. Stand 5 minutes, invert tin onto wire rack, stand further 10 minutes before removing tin. Place cake over tray, while hot, pour Orange Syrup evenly over cake.

Orange Syrup: Combine sugar, water and orange juice in pan, bring to the boil, use while hot.

SPICED PEANUT BISCUITS

These biscuits will keep well stored in an airtight container.

185g unsalted roasted peanuts
¾ cup icing sugar
125g butter
2 teaspoons vanilla
1 cup icing sugar, extra
1 egg, lightly beaten
2 cups plain flour
2 tablespoons cornflour
¼ teaspoon ground cloves
1 egg white, lightly beaten

Process or blend peanuts and icing sugar until coarsely chopped, place on flat tray.

Beat butter, vanilla and extra icing sugar in small bowl with electric mixer until combined, add egg, beat until just combined, transfer mixture to large bowl. Stir in sifted dry ingredients in two batches. Knead dough lightly until smooth, wrap in greaseproof paper, refrigerate 30 minutes. Roll dough between two pieces of plastic wrap or greaseproof paper to thickness of about 1cm. Cut into 1.5cm widths, then cut into 5cm sticks. Brush both sides of sticks with egg white, dip both sides in peanut mixture, place onto greased oven trays, bake in moderate oven 15 minutes, lift onto wire rack to cool.

Makes about 45.

NASI GORENG

You will need to cook two cups of rice for this recipe. Rinse under hot water; drain well, spread out onto absorbent paper or cloth until dry. This can be done a day or two in advance.

500g shelled medium prawns
4 eggs, lightly beaten
2 tablespoons oil
2 cloves garlic, crushed
1 medium onion, finely chopped
1 medium cucumber, finely chopped
2½ cups (250g) bean sprouts, firmly packed
6 cups cooked rice
1 tablespoon sambal oelek
2 tablespoons Ketjap Benteng Asin

Pour eggs into large greased pan, cook until set, remove from pan, cut omelet into thin strips.

Heat oil in wok, add garlic and onion, stir-fry until onion is just soft. Add prawns, cucumber and bean sprouts, stir-fry 1 minute, add rice, sambal oelek and Ketjap Benteng Asin, stir-fry until heated through.

GADO GADO

Vegetables and Peanut Sauce can be prepared several hours ahead of serving time if desired.

500g cauliflower
250g green beans
2 large carrots
2 large potatoes, sliced
1 large cucumber, sliced
5 hard-boiled eggs, quartered
PEANUT SAUCE
2 cups (300g) roasted salted peanuts
410g can coconut milk
1 clove garlic, crushed
2 teaspoons light soy sauce

Cut cauliflower into small flowerets, cut beans and carrots into 2cm lengths. Boil, steam or microwave cauliflower, beans, carrots and potatoes until just tender; drain, rinse under cold water; drain. Combine vegetables with cucumber, decorate with eggs, serve with Peanut Sauce.

Peanut Sauce: Blend or process peanuts until finely crushed. Add coconut milk, garlic and soy sauce, blend all ingredients until smooth.

ABOVE: Gado Gado.

RIGHT: Back: Banana Citrus Cake with Orange Syrup; front: Spiced Peanut Biscuits.

INDONESIAN
DINNER PARTY
FOR FOUR

SEAFOOD WITH BASIL
COCONUT CREAM
SAUCE

MINI SPRING ROLLS

BROCCOLI AND SNOW
PEAS IN SWEET SOY
SAUCE

SPICED KUMARA

LYCHEE MOUSSE

Serve the Spring Rolls either as an entree or as a tasty nibble to have with a drink before dinner. The recipe will make 24 but if this is too many for your purpose, simply freeze the excess, uncooked, for future use. Serve some boiled rice with the main course instead of, or as well as, the vegetable dishes if you prefer. The Lychee Mousse is a delightfully refreshing finish to this meal.

**SEAFOOD WITH BASIL COCONUT
CREAM SAUCE**
500g white fish fillets
500g scallops
500g green prawns
2 tablespoons oil
2 cloves garlic, crushed
1 medium onion, sliced
5cm piece fresh ginger, sliced
4 green shallots, chopped
2 x 400ml cans coconut cream
1 cup fresh basil leaves
½ cup cream
¼ teaspoon turmeric
2 teaspoons plain flour
**2 tablespoons chopped fresh basil,
    extra**
Chop fish into large chunks, shell prawns, leaving tails intact, remove vein, clean scallops. Heat oil in pan, add garlic, onion, ginger and shallots, cook onion until just soft, add coconut cream and basil, bring to the boil stirring constantly, reduce heat, simmer, uncovered, 45 minutes or until re-

duced by half. Strain coconut sauce through fine sieve, discard vegetables. Blend turmeric and flour with cream, add extra basil, stir into sauce, stir over heat until sauce boils and thickens. Steam or poach seafood until just tender; drain, place into serving dish, top with coconut cream sauce.

MINI SPRING ROLLS

Spring rolls can be prepared up to several hours before cooking and serving. Keep covered with a damp cloth. They can also be frozen, uncooked, for a month. Deep fry in frozen state.

**24 small (12cm square) spring roll
    wrappers**
200g can bamboo shoots, drained
2 carrots
2 sticks celery
1 tablespoon oil
1 clove garlic, crushed
**1 small fresh red chilli, finely
    chopped**
½ teaspoon sambal oelek
1 egg white, beaten
oil for deep frying
DIPPING SAUCE
1 teaspoon sambal oelek
1 teaspoon grated fresh ginger
1 tablespoon rice vinegar
1 tablespoon brown sugar
Cut bamboo shoots, carrots and celery into thin strips, about 5cm long. Heat oil in wok, add garlic, chilli and vegetables, stir-fry until vegetables are just soft, stir in sambal oelek, cool to room temperature. Place about a tablespoon of vegetable mixture on one end of spring roll wrapper, fold sides in, brush ends lightly with egg white, roll up firmly; repeat with remaining mixture and wrappers. Deep fry Spring Rolls in hot oil until golden brown; drain on absorbent paper, serve with Dipping Sauce.
Dipping Sauce: Combine all ingredients; mix well.

RIGHT: Back, from left: Broccoli and Snow Peas in Sweet Soy Sauce, Spiced Kumara; front, from left: Seafood with Basil Coconut Cream Sauce, Mini Spring Rolls.

Table from Eastern Emporium, Sydney; painting and batik cloth from Java Bazaar, Paddington, NSW; woven basket with Spiced Kumara and wooden spoon from Gallery Nomad, Paddington, NSW.

BROCCOLI AND SNOW PEAS IN SWEET SOY SAUCE

Ketjap Benteng Asin is a type of sweetened soy sauce.

250g snow peas
250g broccoli
2 tablespoons oil
1 onion, sliced
pinch cinnamon
pinch ground cloves
1 clove garlic, crushed
2 tablespoons Ketjap Benteng Asin

Top and tail snow peas, break broccoli into flowerets. Heat oil in wok, add onion, stir-fry until lightly browned, add cinnamon, cloves, garlic and Ketjap Benteng Asin, add snow peas and broccoli, stir-fry for about 5 minutes or until vegetables are just tender.

SPICED KUMARA

Kumara is an orange-colored sweet potato. The white sweet potato is not a good substitute for this recipe.

2 tablespoons oil
2 kumara, thickly sliced
¼ teaspoon chilli powder
1 tablespoon brown sugar
1 clove garlic, crushed
1 tablespoon lemon juice
1 tablespoon crunchy peanut butter

Heat oil in large pan, add kumara slices in single layer, cook until golden brown on both sides and tender. Gently stir in combined chilli powder, brown sugar, garlic, lemon juice and peanut butter, cook few minutes before serving.

BELOW: Lychee Mousse.

LYCHEE MOUSSE

Mousse can be made up to one day before required if preferred.

2 x 440g cans lychees
3 teaspoons gelatine
1 cup light sour cream
pink food coloring

Drain lychees, reserve ¾ cup syrup. Sprinkle gelatine over reserved syrup, dissolve over hot water (or microwave on HIGH about 30 seconds); cool, but do not allow to set.

Puree lychees in blender or processor, strain, return strained mixture to processor. Add sour cream and gelatine mixture, blend until smooth. Stir in a tiny drop of coloring if desired. Pour into individual serving dishes, refrigerate until set. Serve with whipped cream, extra lychees, glace cherries.

ORIENTAL-STYLE BUFFET FOR 50

WATER CHESTNUTS AND LIVER WITH BACON

SAUSAGES WITH PLUM SAUCE

CREAMY SPICED CHICKEN WINGS

SEAFOOD PLATTER

MARBLED CURRIED EGGS

SNOW PEAS AND MUSHROOM SALAD

KUMARA AND BROCCOLI STIR-FRY

BEEF AND BLACK BEAN CASSEROLE

SWEET AND SOUR CRISPY LENTIL BALLS

TANGY SAFFRON RICE

SESAME AND GINGER CHICKEN SALAD

PEPPERED CHILLI LAMB

NOODLES WITH PORK AND SPINACH

LEMON GLAZED VEGETABLES

QUICK 'N' EASY SINGAPORE PORK

ORANGE CARAMEL BAKED BANANAS

ALMOND COCONUT TRIFLE

MANDARIN MARNIER DELIGHT

A hot or cold weather menu for 50 people with a variety of flavors represented, including sweet and sour, black bean and curry. We have borrowed from many Asian cuisines and combined them for this sumptuous buffet.
There are five mouthwatering ideas for snacks to serve with drinks, five delicious main courses and accompaniments, and three easy, but impressive, desserts. Do-ahead and freezing tips for recipes are included where applicable.
Each recipe in this buffet will serve 10 people generously. We advise you do not make more than the given quantity at one time; domestic kitchen equipment is usually inadequate for large quantity cooking.
Select recipes to suit your taste, allowing one dish for every 10 people. If you want to try the dishes on your family first, simply halve the recipes for an average family. Choose one or both of the punches on page 114 to serve to your guests.

SEAFOOD PLATTER

Prawns and Sauces can be prepared the day before required. Squid can also be prepared, cooked and marinated the day before required.

1½ kg cooked king prawns
500g small squid tubes
DRESSING
2 tablespoons oil
2 tablespoons lime juice
few drops sesame oil
1 teaspoon grated fresh ginger
2 small fresh chillies, chopped
2 teaspoons chopped fresh basil
PEANUT SAUCE
¼ cup smooth peanut butter
½ cup plain yoghurt
¾ cup sour cream
2 teaspoons sate sauce
1 teaspoon ground coriander
SPICY TOMATO SAUCE
2 teaspoons cornflour
1 tablespoon sugar
1 cup water
¼ cup tomato sauce
1 teaspoon light soy sauce
1 tablespoon worcestershire sauce

Peel prawns, leaving tails intact, devein prawns. Slice squid into rings, drop squid into pan of boiling water, boil about 10 seconds or until tender. Drain squid, rinse immediately under cold water; stir in Dressing. Serve prawns with Peanut Sauce and Spicy Tomato Sauce for dipping.
Dressing: Combine all ingredients in jar, shake well.
Peanut Sauce: Stir peanut butter into yoghurt, stir in sour cream, sate sauce and coriander.
Spicy Tomato Sauce: Combine cornflour and sugar in pan, blend in combined water and sauces, stir constantly over heat until the mixture boils and thickens. Serve hot or cold.

WATER CHESTNUTS AND LIVER WITH BACON

May be prepared, ready to grill, about six hours before serving time.

1kg bacon
375g chicken livers
30g butter
310g can water chestnuts, drained

Remove rind from bacon, cut bacon into 10cm lengths. Clean and trim livers. Heat butter in pan, add livers, stir over heat for about 2 minutes or until livers are just tender; drain. Wrap bacon around small pieces of liver and quarters of water chestnuts, secure with toothpicks. Grill until golden brown. Serve immediately.

SAUSAGES WITH PLUM SAUCE

Chinese sausages are available from Asian food shops. Make Plum Sauce up to one week ahead. The Sauce is also delicious with chippolata sausages, simply grill or pan fry them.

500g Chinese sausages
PLUM SAUCE
1 clove garlic, crushed
1 teaspoon grated fresh ginger
3 green shallots, finely chopped
½ x 375ml bottle plum sauce
1 chicken stock cube
1 tablespoon light soy sauce
2 teaspoons cornflour
¼ cup water

Cut sausages into bite-sized pieces. Steam for about 30 minutes; drain on absorbent paper.

Place sausages into a bowl, add a quarter of the Plum Sauce, mix well. Serve with remaining Plum Sauce for dipping.
Plum Sauce: Combine garlic, ginger, shallots, plum sauce, crumbled stock cube, soy sauce in pan, stir in blended cornflour and water, stir constantly over heat until the Sauce boils and thickens. Serve hot or cold.

CREAMY SPICED CHICKEN WINGS

Chicken wings can be prepared a day ahead, covered and refrigerated.

20 chicken wings
2 cups sour cream
1 tablespoon grated fresh ginger
3 cloves garlic, crushed
1 tablespoon curry powder
tiny pinch saffron powder
½ teaspoon chilli powder
1 teaspoon garam masala

Cut chicken wings into 3 at joints, discard wing tips. Combine sour cream, ginger, garlic, curry, saffron, chilli and garam masala in bowl, add chicken, mix well. Place chicken in baking dish in single layer, bake in moderately hot oven 30 minutes or until golden brown, serve hot.

ABOVE: Back: Water Chestnuts with Liver and Bacon; front: Sausages with Plum Sauce.
RIGHT: Back: Seafood Platter; front, from left: Spicy Tomato Sauce, Peanut Sauce.
BELOW: Creamy Spiced Chicken Wings.

MARBLED CURRIED EGGS

Stirring the eggs before they boil will centralise the egg yolks.

10 small eggs
½ cup turmeric
2 tablespoons plain yoghurt
1 teaspoon curry powder

Place eggs in large pan in single layer. Cover eggs with cold water, stir constantly but gently over high heat until water comes to the boil. Reduce heat, boil gently, uncovered, for 8 minutes; drain. Lightly crack egg shells all over with a teaspoon. Place enough water in the same pan to cover the eggs when they are added later. Stir in turmeric. Bring turmeric water to the boil, gently add eggs, simmer 5 minutes. Drain eggs, return eggs to pan, add enough cold water to cover, stand 1 hour.

Remove shells, cut eggs in half, remove yolks. Combine yolks, yoghurt and curry powder, mash well, push through a fine sieve. Pipe mixture into egg white halves, decorate.

SNOW PEAS AND MUSHROOM SALAD

May be prepared, covered and refrigerated up to several hours ahead.

500g snow peas
500g baby mushrooms, sliced
2 red peppers, chopped
HONEY DRESSING
½ cup oil
¼ cup white vinegar
1 teaspoon honey
1 teaspoon grated fresh ginger
½ teaspoon sambal oelek

Top and tail snow peas. Drop snow peas into pan of boiling water, drain immediately; rinse under cold water; drain, place in bowl.

Combine mushrooms and peppers in separate bowl. Pour two thirds of the Honey Dressing over mushrooms and remaining Dressing over snow peas, mix well. Place snow peas on platter with mushroom mixture.

Honey Dressing: Combine all ingredients in screw-top jar, shake well.

ABOVE: Marbled Curried Eggs.
BELOW: Snow Peas and Mushroom Salad.

Blue background is Windsor Blue from Laminex Industries, Sydney.

KUMARA AND BROCCOLI STIR-FRY

Have kumara cooled and remaining ingredients prepared for last minute stir-frying as close to serving as possible.

4 kumara, thickly sliced
¼ cup oil
2 onions, coarsely chopped
8 green shallots, chopped
1 clove garlic, crushed
½ teaspoon five spice powder
1 bunch Chinese broccoli, chopped
5 cups (500g) bean sprouts
1 teaspoon cornflour
1½ cups chicken stock

Boil, steam or microwave kumara until tender; drain.

Heat oil in pan or wok, add onions, stir-fry few minutes or until just tender. Add shallots, garlic and five spice powder, stir-fry 1 minute. Add broccoli, bean sprouts and kumara, stir-fry until broccoli is just tender. Stir in blended cornflour and stock, stir constantly until mixture boils and thickens.

BEEF AND BLACK BEAN CASSEROLE

Casserole can be made up to two days before required or frozen for up to one month ahead.

2kg rump steak, sliced
¼ cup dry sherry
¼ cup light soy sauce
3 tablespoons canned black beans
2 teaspoons sugar
3 teaspoons water
3 tablespoons oil
3 onions, chopped
2 red peppers, chopped
230g can sliced bamboo shoots, drained
3 teaspoons curry powder
2 tablespoons cornflour
4 cups water, extra

Combine steak, sherry and soy sauce in bowl, cover, marinate 1 hour. Place black beans in bowl, cover with water, stand 20 minutes; drain, rinse under cold water. Drain beans, place on plate, mash with sugar and water.

Heat 2 tablespoons of the oil in pan or wok, add onions, stir-fry few minutes, add peppers, bamboo shoots and curry powder, stir-fry for 1 minute, place into deep ovenproof dish.

Heat the remaining 1 tablespoon oil in pan or wok, add a quarter of the steak, stir-fry until well browned all over, place into ovenproof dish. Repeat with remaining steak. Add bean mixture, blended cornflour and extra water and any remaining marinade to pan or wok. Stir constantly over heat until mixture boils and thickens, pour over steak, mix well, cover, bake in moderate oven about 1 hour or until the steak is tender.

SWEET AND SOUR CRISPY LENTIL BALLS

Lentil balls can be deep fried up to eight hours ahead of serving if desired. Reheat lentil balls in an ovenproof dish in single layer, bake, covered with foil with slashed holes to allow steam to escape, in moderate oven for about 30 minutes. Sweet and Sour Sauce can be prepared the day before required and reheated in pan when ready to serve. This Sauce is ideal for serving over chicken, seafood, pork and beef.

6 x 300g cans soy beans
2 cloves garlic, crushed
1 large onion, finely chopped
3 teaspoons grated fresh ginger
¼ cup chopped parsley
⅓ cup plain flour
1½ teaspoons ground coriander
3 teaspoons light soy sauce
oil for deep frying

BELOW: Back, from left: Beef and Black Bean Casserole, Sweet and Sour Crispy Lentil Balls; front: Kumara and Broccoli Stir-Fry.

SWEET AND SOUR SAUCE

440g can unsweetened pineapple pieces
1 tablespoon cornflour
1 tablespoon oil
1 large red pepper, chopped
2 sticks celery, chopped
¾ cup water
2 tablespoons tomato sauce
230g can sliced bamboo shoots, drained
4 green shallots, chopped

Drain and rinse beans, mash well with a fork or partly puree in blender or processor. Stir in garlic, onion, ginger, parsley, flour, coriander and soy sauce. Roll into about 30 balls, deep fry in hot oil until golden brown; drain. Serve immediately topped with hot Sweet and Sour Sauce.

Sweet and Sour Sauce: Drain pineapple, reserve juice, blend juice with cornflour. Heat oil in pan or wok, add pepper and celery, stir-fry 2 minutes. Add blended pineapple juice to pan with water, tomato sauce, bamboo shoots and pineapple, stir constantly over heat until mixture boils and thickens. Stir in shallots just before serving.

SESAME AND GINGER CHICKEN SALAD

Salad can be prepared completely up to 12 hours ahead of serving time. Store, covered, in refrigerator.

10 chicken breast fillets
2½ cups chicken stock
1 red pepper
1 carrot
425g can whole baby corn, drained
4 green shallots, chopped
3 sticks celery, chopped
2 tablespoons toasted sesame
  seeds
MARINADE
¼ cup light soy sauce
2 tablespoons dry sherry
1 tablespoon honey
2 teaspoons grated fresh ginger
2 cloves garlic, crushed
½ teaspoon sesame oil
DRESSING
3cm piece fresh ginger
½ cup oil
¼ cup white vinegar
2 tablespoons dry sherry
1 tablespoon light soy sauce
2 tablespoons honey
½ teaspoon sesame oil

Place chicken in large bowl, add Marinade, cover, refrigerate several hours or overnight.

Remove chicken from Marinade. Place stock in pan, bring to the boil, add chicken, cover, simmer 10 minutes or until chicken is just tender; drain,

TANGY SAFFRON RICE

This rice dish can be served hot or cold; if serving cold, it can be prepared up to a day before serving.

250g bottle Chinese mixed pickles
3 cups long grain rice
½ teaspoon ground cardamom
½ teaspoon ground cinnamon
¼ teaspoon saffron powder
1 teaspoon oil
1 cup (125g) slivered almonds
1 cup (100g) bean sprouts
1 large red pepper, chopped
DRESSING
¼ cup oil
½ teaspoon sesame oil

Drain pickles, reserve ⅓ cup liquid for Dressing; chop pickles. Bring a large pan of water to the boil, add rice, cardamom, cinnamon and saffron. Boil rapidly, uncovered, for 10 minutes or until rice is tender; drain. Spread rice evenly onto tray, cool.

Heat oil in pan or wok, add almonds, stir-fry until lightly browned; drain. Add rice to pan, stir-fry until heated through, add pickles, bean sprouts and pepper. Stir in Dressing and almonds, stir-fry until heated through.

Dressing: Combine reserved pickled liquid and remaining ingredients in screw-top jar, shake well.

108

cool. Cut chicken into strips. Cut pepper and carrot into thin strips about 5cm long. Cut corn into quarters lengthways. Combine chicken with vegetables and Dressing, sprinkle with sesame seeds.

Marinade: Combine all ingredients, mix well.

Dressing: Finely grate ginger, press between two teaspoons over screwtop jar to extract juice, discard ginger pieces. Add remaining ingredients to jar, shake well.

PEPPERED CHILLI LAMB

Ask butcher to bone out loins of lamb for you and to leave a large flap so they are easy to roll. Crush peppercorns coarsely in bag with hammer or meat mallet. Lamb can be served hot or cold. If serving hot, stand cooked lamb for 20 minutes before slicing. If serving cold, cool to room temperature, then refrigerate before slicing — lamb can be cooked the day before in this case.

2 x 1½kg loins of lamb
½ cup crushed black peppercorns
MARINADE
2 cloves garlic, crushed
1 small fresh red chilli, finely chopped
¼ cup dry sherry
¼ cup light soy sauce
¼ cup sate sauce
¼ cup oil
Trim fat from lamb, roll up, tie firmly with string to hold in shape during cooking. Place lamb in Marinade, cover, refrigerate overnight. Drain lamb, reserve Marinade. Roll lamb in peppercorns, place on rack over baking dish. Bake in hot oven 10 minutes, reduce heat to moderate, bake further 35 to 45 minutes or until cooked as desired. Baste with reserved Marinade several times during cooking.

Marinade: Combine all ingredients; mix well.

NOODLES WITH PORK AND SPINACH

This recipe is best cooked as close to serving time as possible.

500g fresh egg noodles
2 bunches English spinach
250g barbecued pork, chopped
2 tablespoons oil
1 clove garlic, crushed
1 small fresh red chilli, finely chopped
1 tablespoon cornflour
¼ cup water
¼ cup oyster sauce
¼ cup dry sherry
Cook noodles in boiling water for 2 minutes; drain. Remove leaves from spinach stems.

Heat oil in pan or wok, add garlic and chilli, stir-fry 1 minute, add spinach and pork, stir-fry 2 minutes. Add noodles, then combined blended cornflour

and water, oyster sauce and sherry, cook, stirring constantly, until mixture boils and thickens, serve immediately.

LEMON GLAZED VEGETABLES

Vegetables are best cooked as near to serving time as possible. The glaze can be made 12 hours ahead and reheated just before serving over vegetables.

1kg baby new potatoes
1 small (1kg) cauliflower
750g broccoli
LEMON GLAZE
30g butter
1 clove garlic, crushed
2 tablespoons sugar
¼ teaspoon ground ginger
¼ teaspoon ground coriander
2 tablespoons cornflour
2 cups chicken stock
2 tablespoons lemon juice
1 tablespoon dry sherry
Peel and halve potatoes, boil, steam or microwave until tender; drain. Cut cauliflower and broccoli into flowerets, boil, steam or microwave until tender; drain. Place vegetables on serving dish, top with Lemon Glaze.

Lemon Glaze: Melt butter in pan, add garlic, sugar, ginger and coriander, stir over heat 1 minute. Gradually stir in blended cornflour and stock, lemon juice and sherry, stir constantly over heat until mixture boils and thickens.

QUICK 'N' EASY SINGAPORE PORK

Singapore Mild Curry Sauce is an imported product available in delicatessens and gourmet sections of large supermarkets. This recipe can be prepared up to 12 hours before serving, it will also freeze for up to one month.

2½kg pork fillets, sliced
1 tablespoon oil
2 cloves garlic, crushed
2 onions, chopped
1 tablespoon grated fresh ginger
2 x 375kg cans Singapore Mild Curry Sauce
2 x 415g cans coconut cream
½ cup tomato sauce
¼ cup brown sugar
1 stem lemon grass, coarsely chopped
Heat oil in pan or wok, add garlic and onions, stir-fry 1 minute, add ginger, stir-fry 1 minute, add Curry Sauce, coconut cream, tomato sauce, brown sugar and lemon grass. Bring to the boil, reduce heat, simmer 15 minutes, add pork, simmer, uncovered, about 30 minutes or until mixture is thick. Remove lemon grass before serving.

TOP LEFT: Back: Sesame and Ginger Chicken Salad; front: Tangy Saffron Rice.
LEFT: Back: Peppered Chilli Lamb; front: Noodles with Pork and Spinach.
ABOVE: Back: Quick 'n' Easy Singapore Pork; front: Lemon Glazed Vegetables.

ALMOND COCONUT TRIFLE

Can be made up to two days ahead of serving time if desired. Decorate several hours before serving.

450g madeira or butter cake
¾ cup sweet sherry
2 x 100g packets raspberry flavored
   jelly crystals
1½ cups boiling water
375ml can evaporated skim milk
1 teaspoon almond essence
2 x 300ml cartons thickened cream
fresh fruit
toasted, shredded coconut
COCONUT CUSTARD
8 egg yolks
½ cup cornflour
1½ cups castor sugar
3 cups milk
300ml carton thickened cream
1 teaspoon coconut essence

Line base of large shallow dish with slices of cake, sprinkle evenly with sherry. Place jelly crystals into bowl, add boiling water, stir until crystals are dissolved. Stir in milk and almond essence; refrigerate until almost set. Pour jelly over cake, refrigerate until set. Spread Coconut Custard evenly over jelly, refrigerate until set. Decorate trifle with whipped cream, fruit and coconut.

Coconut Custard: Mix egg yolks, cornflour and sugar together in large pan, gradually stir in milk. Stir constantly over heat until mixture boils and thickens, pour into large bowl, cover surface with plastic wrap to prevent skin forming, cool to room temperature. Whip cream and coconut essence until soft peaks form, fold into Custard in two batches.

ORANGE CARAMEL BAKED BANANAS

May be prepared, ready to cook, up to 30 minutes beforehand.

90g butter
¾ cup brown sugar, firmly packed
2 tablespoons lemon juice
⅓ cup orange juice
⅓ cup Grand Marnier
2 teaspoons cornflour
1 tablespoon water
10 firm ripe bananas, chopped
½ cup flaked almonds, toasted

Melt butter in pan, add sugar, stir until sugar is dissolved. Add lemon juice, orange juice and Grand Marnier, bring to the boil, stir in blended cornflour and water, stir until mixture boils and thickens. Place bananas in shallow ovenproof dish, pour sauce over bananas, bake, uncovered, in moderate oven 20 minutes or until bananas are just tender. Serve topped with almonds and whipped cream or icecream.

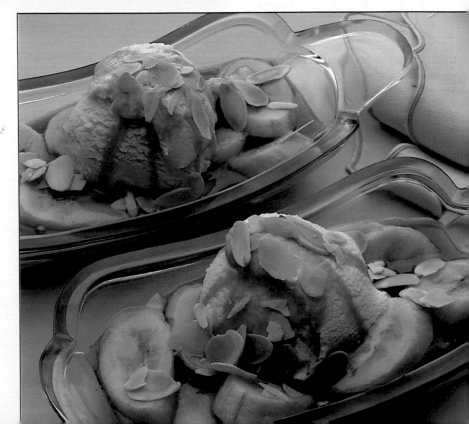

MANDARIN MARNIER DELIGHT

May be made the day before required, covered and refrigerated.

¾ cup water
3 tablespoons gelatine
⅓ cup plain flour
2 cups sugar
1½ cups water, extra
3 teaspoons grated mandarin rind
2¼ cups mandarin juice
¼ cup Grand Marnier
5 egg whites
few drops orange food coloring

Place water in bowl, sprinkle with gelatine, stir, place bowl over a pan of hot water, stir over heat until gelatine is dissolved, (or microwave on HIGH for about 1 minute); stand 30 minutes.

Combine flour and sugar in pan, gradually stir in extra water, stir constantly over heat until mixture boils and thickens, cover surface of mixture to prevent skin forming; stand 30 minutes. Beat combined gelatine and flour mixtures in large bowl with electric mixer for about 10 minutes or until mixture thickens. Stir in mandarin rind and juice, and Grand Marnier. Beat egg whites in small bowl with electric mixer until soft peaks form, gently fold into mandarin mixture with food coloring. Pour into serving bowl, refrigerate until set. Serve topped with whipped cream and extra mandarins.

TOP LEFT: Almond Coconut Trifle.
BELOW LEFT: Orange Caramel Baked Bananas.
BELOW: Mandarin Marnier Delight.

COCKTAILS
THE COOL TOUCH

BELOW: From left: Melon Mindbender, Mandarin Cooler, Oriental Blossom.
RIGHT: Clockwise from front: Lychee Cointreau Cocktail, Creamy Banana Delight, Strawberry Sling, Mango Daiquiri, Sake Stinger.

All glasses from Studio Haus, Sydney; Melon Mindbender glass is Black Line from Kosta Boda, Sydney.

We have broken with Asian tradition again by providing recipes for drinks before or during the meal. Some Asian cultures refrain from anything alcoholic; others do allow wine or spirits. We suggest serving wine — a rosé is an excellent choice. Before the meal try one of our exotic cocktails. Make sure that all the ingredients are icy cold before mixing the drinks. Serve cocktails immediately after mixing.

MELON MINDBENDER

ORIENTAL BLOSSOM

MANGO DAIQUIRI

LYCHEE COINTREAU COCKTAIL

SAKE STINGER

MANDARIN COOLER

STRAWBERRY SLING

CREAMY BANANA DELIGHT

PEACHY CHAMPAGNE MARNIER PUNCH

ORANGE PEKOE TEA PUNCH

MELON MINDBENDER

Midori is a melon based liqueur

¼ honeydew melon (about 400g)
1 tablespoon midori
1 tablespoon vodka
¼ cup cream
crushed ice

Blend or process melon, midori, vodka and cream until smooth and creamy. Pour into glass, serve immediately over crushed ice.
  Serves 1.

ORIENTAL BLOSSOM

Malibu is a coconut and rum flavored drink available in 700ml bottles.

2 tablespoons Malibu coconut liqueur
1 tablespoon white rum
1 tablespoon curacao
½ cup sweetened pineapple juice
2 tablespoons canned coconut cream
2 large ice cubes

Blend or process all ingredients until ice is crushed; serve immediately.
  Makes 1 large serving.

MANGO DAIQUIRI
1 large ripe mango
2 tablespoons lemon juice
½ cup white rum
2 tablespoons sugar
4 large ice cubes
Blend or process all ingredients until smooth. Serve immediately.
    Serves 2.

LYCHEE COINTREAU COCKTAIL
565g can lychees
1 teaspoon grenadine syrup
½ cup cointreau
⅓ cup cream
6 large ice cubes
Blend or process undrained lychees with remaining ingredients until smooth. Strain before serving immediately in glasses.
    Serves 4.

SAKE STINGER
1 tablespoon sake
1 tablespoon lime juice
1 teaspoon castor sugar
crushed ice
soda water
Shake sake, lime juice, sugar and crushed ice together in cocktail shaker. Pour immediately into frosted glass, top up with soda water.
Note: To frost a glass, dip rim of glass into unbeaten egg white, then sugar.
    Serves 1.

MANDARIN COOLER
1 tablespoon mandarin liqueur
1 tablespoon lemon juice
¼ cup canned apricot nectar
crushed ice
Shake mandarin liqueur, lemon juice, apricot nectar and crushed ice together in cocktail shaker. Pour immediately into serving glass.
    Serves 1.

STRAWBERRY SLING
½ x 250g punnet strawberries
1 tablespoon gin
1 tablespoon kirsch
¼ cup lemonade
crushed ice
Blend or process hulled strawberries, gin and kirsch until smooth. Place crushed ice in glass, add strawberry mixture, top with lemonade, serve immediately.
    Serves 1.

CREAMY BANANA DELIGHT
2 tablespoons banana liqueur
1 tablespoon white rum
1 small very ripe banana
½ cup cream
tiny drop of yellow food coloring
2 large ice cubes
Blend or process all ingredients until ice is crushed.
    Makes 1 serving.

PEACHY CHAMPAGNE MARNIER PUNCH

This punch is extravagantly delicious. Make about half the quantity of punch at a time to retain the sparkle of the champagne. Make sure all ingredients are icy cold. Add fresh fruit of your choice just before serving.

700ml bottle Grand Marnier
2 litres orange juice
2 x 850ml cans peach nectar
8 x 750ml bottles champagne

Combine all ingredients in a large punch bowl just before serving. Add ice if desired.

Makes about 10 litres.

ORANGE PEKOE TEA PUNCH

This is a refreshing non alcoholic punch; make sure all ingredients are icy cold.

2 tablespoons orange pekoe tea
2 litres (8 cups) boiling water
2 cups lemon juice
2 cups lime juice
4 cups sugar
4 x 850g cans sweetened crushed pineapple
1½ litres orange juice
2 cups lemon juice, extra
1 pineapple
1 cucumber, peeled, sliced

Pour the boiling water over tea in bowl, stand 10 minutes; strain tea through fine sieve or cloth; cool to room temperature. Combine lemon juice, lime juice and sugar in pan, stir over heat until sugar is dissolved; bring to the boil, reduce heat, simmer, uncovered, 5 minutes, cool to room temperature. Add tea, undrained crushed pineapple, orange juice and extra lemon juice. Refrigerate before serving with chunks of pineapple, cucumber slices and ice.

Makes about 10 litres.

BELOW: From left: Peachy Champagne Marnier Punch, Orange Pekoe Tea Punch.

Tea punch bowl, glasses and ladle are Krosno from K.W.L. Imports, Sydney; champagne punch bowl is Krosno from Studio Haus, Sydney.

GLOSSARY

Many ingredients and terms used in Asian cooking are unfamiliar to some of us. This illustrated glossary is designed to help you recognise ingredients and master preparation techniques.

Agar-agar: is made from different types of seaweed. It has excellent setting properties, similar to gelatine, and will set at room temperature. ▼

Asparagus: to prepare this delicious vegetable it is better if the little nodules are scraped from the ends (not the tips) of the stalks; we use a vegetable peeler to do this. Cut or snap off the fibrous part of the stem before cooking. ▶

Bean sauce: we used Pun Chun brand in a 375ml jar; it contains soy beans, flour and salt. Bean paste or soy bean sauce can also be used.

Beans, green and snake: we used two types of green beans in this book; one can be substituted for the other. Green or French beans should be topped and tailed before use; the snake beans need to be chopped. ▼

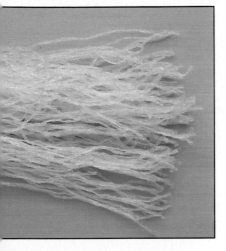

Bamboo shoots: the young tender shoots of bamboo plants are available in cans. They are mainly used to add texture to food.

Bamboo skewers: can be used instead of metal skewers if they are soaked in water overnight or several hours beforehand to prevent burning during cooking. They are available in several different lengths. ▼

Barbecued pork: roasted pork fillets available from many Asian fresh food and specialty stores. ▶

Beef: we used several different cuts throughout the book; usually the tender cuts such as fillet or rump are ideal for quick cooking. If the recipe requires the beef to be sliced finely, freeze the piece for at least 30 minutes before cutting. Cut across the grain of the meat (as shown) for maximum flavor and moisture retention during cooking. ▼

Bicarbonate of soda: also known as baking soda.

Black beans: are fermented, salted soy beans. We used both canned and dried; one can be substituted for the other. Drain and rinse the canned variety, soak and rinse the dried variety, leftover beans will keep well for months in an airtight jar in the refrigerator. Mash beans when cooking to release the flavor.

Black fungus: is a type of wild mushroom which is sold dried and packaged. Picture shows two varieties before and after soaking. ▲

Blanching: is usually required when the cooking of the food is minimal, as in snow peas or lettuce, or when an ingredient needs to be lightly cooked before a longer cooking process takes place. This is often the case before vegetables are stir-fried.

Bring a pan of water to the boil, add the specified ingredient, then follow individual recipe instructions. After the ingredient is drained it should be placed into a bowl of iced water, or rinsed under cold water until the ingredient is cold, according to the individual recipe.

Bonito, dried flakes: bonito is fish from the mackerel family. It is available in dried flaked form, and is an ingredient of Japanese dashi.

Broccoli: our picture shows broccoli broken into flowerets, and scraping and slicing stems ready for cooking. Stems are just as tasty as flowerets but require longer cooking. ▼

Broccoli, Chinese (gai lum): remove and discard the fibrous parts of the stems, cut flowerets away from stems and leaves. If using remaining stems, peel away any tough skin with a vegetable peeler and chop stems. ▶

Butter: we used salted and unsalted (sweet) butter in this book.

Cabbage, Chinese (wong nga baak): remove, wash, shred or chop leaves and braise, steam or stir-fry. It can be used as a substitute for ordinary English cabbage. ▼

Cabbage, Chinese flowering (cho sum): the whole cabbage can be used; it is usually boiled, steamed or stir-fried. ▼

Caraway seeds: a member of the parsley family, it is available in seed or ground form and can be used in sweet and savory dishes.

Cardamom: an expensive spice with an exotic fragrance. It can be bought in pod, seed or ground form. You can grind your own cardamom from the seeds in a mortar and pestle.

Chicken: our picture shows how to chop an uncooked chicken the traditional Chinese way. ▲

Chillies, fresh and dried: are available in many different types and sizes. The small ones (bird's eye or bird peppers) are the hottest. Use tight-fitting gloves when handling and chopping fresh chillies as they can burn your skin. The seeds are the hottest part of the chillies so remove them if you want to reduce the heat content of recipes. ▼

Chilli powder: the Asian variety of the powder is the hottest and is made from ground dried chillies; it can be used as a substitute for fresh chillies in the proportion of ½ teaspoon ground chilli powder to 1 medium chopped chilli.

Chilli sauce: we used a hot Chinese variety. It consists of chillies, salt and vinegar. We used it sparingly so that you can easily increase amounts in recipes to suit your taste.

116

Chinese chard (bok choy):
remove and discard stems, use leaves
and young tender parts of stems. It
requires only a short cooking time;
add to soups or stir-fry. ▼

Chinese mixed pickles:
consist of a variety of fruit and
vegetables preserved in vinegar,
sugar and salt. The ingredients in the
jar we used were ginger, shallots,
pawpaws, cucumbers, carrots, chilli
and pears. ▼

Chopsticks: are used traditionally
to eat Chinese and many other Asian
countries' food. Japanese chopsticks
(shown on chopsticks stand) are
slightly different: they are smooth and
more pointed than the Chinese type.

Chopsticks can be made from all
kinds of exotic material but the most
common are wood and plastic. Very
long chopsticks are available for use
as a cooking utensil. Picture shows
how to hold the chopsticks. ▲

Cinnamon: can be bought in dried
sticks or ground form. It is used in
both sweet and savory recipes.

Cleaver: readily available in many
sizes and types. They are inexpensive
and take only a little practice to use
efficiently. Steel cleavers need to be
wrapped in an oiled cloth to prevent
them from rusting; keep them razor
sharp by sharpening on an oilstone.

Coconut: we used both canned
coconut cream and milk; one can be
substituted for the other. As a rule,
the cream is thicker than the milk, but
different brands vary quite a lot.
Coconut cream is also available in
200ml cardboard cartons and 200g
blocks of pure creamed coconut.

Follow directions on the blocks.
It is easy to make your own milk
using desiccated coconut. (Coconut
milk is not the liquid inside the mature
coconut).

Place 2 cups desiccated coconut
into a bowl, cover with 2½ cups hot
water, stand until mixture is just
warm, mix with the hand, then strain
through a fine sieve or cloth,
squeezing out as much liquid as you
can. This will give you about 1½ cups
thick milk, this can be used when
canned coconut cream is specified.
The same coconut can be used again;
simply add another 2½ cups hot
water, and continue as above, this will
give you a watery milk. This can be
combined with the first thicker milk
and is a good substitute for the
canned coconut milk specified in our
recipes. It can also be blended or
processed for about 20 seconds, then
strained as above.

Coconut can be bought as fresh
mature coconuts, or dried,
desiccated, shredded or flaked.
See Toasting for how to toast.

Coriander: also known as Cilantro
and Chinese parsley, is essential to
many south-east Asian cuisines; its
seeds are the main ingredient of curry
powder. A strongly flavored herb, use
it sparingly until you are accustomed
to the unique flavor. Parsley can be
used as a substitute; it looks the
same but tastes quite different.
Coriander is available fresh, ground
and in seed form.

Cornflour: also known as
cornstarch, is the main thickening
ingredient used in Chinese cooking. It
is always blended with a liquid before
being added to other ingredients,
then boiled until the mixture thickens;
this boiling eliminates the starchy
taste. Cornflour gives the
characteristic opaque sauces
associated with Chinese food.

Chives: See onions.

Chopping diagonally: this
method of chopping is used to
preserve the color, flavor and texture
of the vegetables. Picture shows the
correct way to chop, using either a
cleaver or a sharp knife. ▶

Cream: we used a pouring light cream (also known as half 'n' half) and thickened cream, when specified, in this book.

Cumin: is available in seed or ground form; it is another important component of curry powder.

Curry leaves: these are available in fresh or dried form.

Curry powder: a convenient combination of spices in powdered form. This is not used in countries where curry is eaten daily, there the spices are ground individually and combined in endless variations.

All our recipes tend to be mild in curry flavor rather than hot; the heat can be increased by adding more chilli in the form of sauce or fresh or dried powder. Curry powder consists of chilli, coriander, cumin, fennel, fenugreek and turmeric in varying proportions. Buy curry powder in small quantities in airtight containers from a shop which specialises in these ingredients.

Daikon: a basic food in Japan, it is also called the giant white radish. Daikon is similar in taste to a very tender young turnip which can be used as a substitute. Daikon can be grated and eaten raw, boiled, steamed, stewed or stir-fried. ▼

Dashi: is a basic fish and seaweed stock responsible for the distinctive flavor of Japanese food. It is made from dried bonito flakes and konbu. Instant dashi, a good substitute, is readily available. Dashi is used as a stock, soup, or as an ingredient in dipping sauces.

Dried yellow mung beans: dried mung beans, complete with husks, are green and tiny and used for sprouting (right). The husks are removed and the bean is actually yellow when dried to use in cooking (left). Flour and a variety of noodles are also made from these beans. ▶

Dry sherry: we used dry sherry instead of traditional Chinese rice wine in our recipes.

Eggplant: a purple fruit, also known as aubergine.

Essence: also known as extract. We used almond, coconut and vanilla essence which are available from health food stores. We also used jasmine essence which is available from Asian food stores.

Fennel: has a slight aniseed taste when fresh, ground or in seed form. Fennel seeds are a component of curry powder.

Fish sauce: is an essential ingredient in the cooking of a number of Asian countries including Thailand and Vietnam. It is made from the liquid drained from salted, fermented anchovies.

Five spice powder: a pungent mixture of ground spices which include cinnamon, cloves, fennel, star anise and Szechwan pepper.

Frying: there are three types of frying used throughout this book.
1. Deep frying: can be done in a wok or a deep wide pan. There must be enough oil, so that the food can be completely submerged; and will not require turning. The oil must be hot to prevent the food absorbing the oil. Most deep fried food is cooked quickly; there are some exceptions, follow individual recipes.
2. Shallow frying: is done in a wide-topped heavy-based pan or wok with enough oil to come about halfway up the side of the food. Heat the pan, add the oil, then heat the oil before adding the food. Food which is shallow fried requires slower, more gentle cooking and turning at least once during the cooking time.
3. Stir-frying: can be done in a wok, or large wide-topped heavy-based pan. Heat the wok or pan before adding the oil. Only a little oil is used for stir-frying and it must be very hot before the food is added. The food to be stir-fried is usually chopped finely to allow flavor and color retention

during the short, hot cooking process. As the name implies the food is stirred and lifted all the time it is cooking. If using a wok, a wok chan fits perfectly; if using a pan, use an egg slide, fork or wooden spoon; do not squash the food while stir-frying.

Galangal: is the dried root of a plant of the ginger family. It is used as a flavoring, and is either removed before serving or left uneaten.

Garam masala: there are many variations of the combinations of cardamom, cinnamon, cloves, coriander, cumin and nutmeg used to make up this spice used often in Indian cooking. Sometimes pepper is used to make a hot variation. Garam masala is readily available in jars in Asian food stores.

Garlic: is used extensively in all Asian cooking. Picture shows from top left: a knob and cloves of garlic; in centre: sliced, slivered and chopped garlic; from top at right: a peeled clove and garlic mixed with salt and crushed with the flat of a cleaver or a broad knife. ▼

Garnishes: easy steps to making some of the garnishes used in this book are pictured opposite. ▶

Ghee (clarified butter): a pure butter fat available in cans, it can be heated to high temperatures without burning because of the lack of salts and milk solids.

It is easy to make your own ghee. Heat butter in a pan until it is melted and becomes frothy. Remove foam from top with a spoon. Pour butter into a bowl, discard solid bits and pieces remaining in the pan. Cool butter to room temperature then refrigerate until set. Lift the fat from the top, leaving the solids underneath. Heat the fat, strain through a fine cloth to remove any remaining solids; it is now ready to use.

Ginger: picture shows a piece of ▶ fresh (green or root) ginger; scrape away outside skin and it is ready to grate, chop or slice as required.

Fresh, peeled ginger can be preserved in dry sherry, enough to cover; keep in airtight jar in refrigerator. Sliced pickled ginger is used as a garnish for the classic Japanese sushi. It is preserved in rice vinegar and sugar. Red ginger is dyed and mainly used as a garnish.

Ground ginger is also available, but should not be substituted for fresh ginger in any recipe.

Green ginger wine: an Australian made alcoholic sweet wine infused with finely ground ginger.

Green shallots: see onions (also known as scallions and spring onions); do not confuse with the small brown shallots. Picture shows from top: shallot, trimmed and ready to use; centre, from left: sticks, shredded sticks, curls; bottom, from left: shallots shredded, chopped diagonally and chopped through. ▼

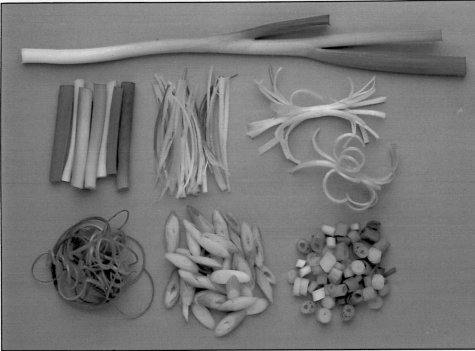

ABOVE: Tomato Rose.

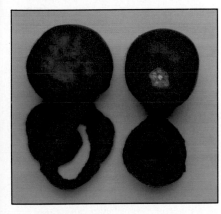

ABOVE: Cucumber garnishes.
BELOW: Carrot and Cucumber, peeled.

ABOVE: Lemon twigs and loops.
BELOW: Orange segments.

Grill, griller: broil or broiler.

Hoisin sauce: is a thick sweet Chinese barbecue sauce made from a mixture of salted black beans, onions and garlic.

Icing sugar: also known as confectioners' or powdered sugar.

Kaffir lime leaves: also known as citrus or lime leaves, are bought in dried form and give a unique flavor to Thai and Malaysian food.

Ketjap Bentang Asin: a sweet spicy soy sauce-based ketchup used in Indonesian recipes.

Kiwi fruit: a green fruit, also known as Chinese gooseberry. ▼

Konbu: is kelp seaweed used in Japanese cooking — as an ingredient in dashi, to flavor rice for sushi, and also as a relish.

Kumara: is an orange-colored sweet potato. ▼

Lemon grass: fresh lemon grass is readily available from Asian food stores and needs to be bruised or chopped before using to release flavor. Follow individual recipes. Fresh lemon grass will keep in a jug of water at room temperature for several weeks; the water must be changed daily. It can be bought dried; to reconstitute: place several pieces of dried lemon grass in a bowl, cover with hot water, stand 20 minutes; drain; it is now ready to use. This amount is a substitute for one stem of fresh lemon grass. ▲

Lentils: there are many different types of lentils; all require overnight soaking before cooking with the exception of red lentils which are ready for cooking without soaking.

Lettuce cups: a good shape can be obtained by trimming lettuce leaves with scissors. Wash and dry lettuce before cutting; store in refrigerator until ready to use. ▼

Lotus root: is available in cans, or dried form which needs soaking in hot water with a dash of lemon juice for about 20 minutes. Fresh lotus root is occasionally available.

Lychees: delicious fruit with a light texture and flavor; peel away the rough skin, remove the seed and use. They are also available in cans. ▶

Maltose: a sugar extract used for flavoring and coloring.

Marinade: marinating is used to impart as much flavor as possible into food. It is also used as a method of tenderising food, usually meat. Marinating can be done in 30 minutes or up to 2 days, depending on individual recipes.

Mint: there are many varieties of mint; the one most used in Asian cooking is the round leaf variety.

Mirin: is a sweet rice wine, golden in color and low in alcohol, used in Japanese cooking. Substitute 1 teaspoon sugar and 1 teaspoon dry sherry for each 1 tablespoon mirin.

Miso: a fermented soy bean paste which comes in many colors, textures, flavors and aromas. Keep covered in refrigerator.

Mushrooms: pictured right, some of the mushrooms available. Clockwise from front right: dried mushrooms, unique in flavor; soak in hot water, cover, for about 20 minutes, remove and discard stems, use caps as directed in individual recipes; oyster, also known as abalone mushrooms; small fresh cultivated mushrooms; straw mushrooms, available in cans (champignons can be substituted); champignons, small, cultivated canned mushrooms. ▶

Mustard seeds: the tiny black variety is more potent than the large yellow seeds.

Noodles: picture at bottom of page shows some of the wide variety of noodles available for Asian cooking. ▼

Nori: is a type of dried seaweed used in Japanese cooking as a flavoring, garnish or for sushi. Sold in thin sheets, it must be crispened by heating over a flame or in the oven to seal in the flavor before using.

Oil: peanut oil is the most commonly used oil in Asian cooking, however a lighter salad type of oil can be used.

Omelet: picture shows an omelet being cooked in a wok, then being rolled and sliced for use. Sometimes a little water is added to the lightly beaten eggs just before cooking to make the omelet lighter. ▼

Mussels: should be bought from a fish market where there is reliably fresh fish. They must be tightly closed when bought, indicating they are alive. Before cooking, scrub the shells with a strong brush and remove the "beards". Discard any shells that do not open after cooking. ▼

Back from left: fresh egg noodles, rice noodles (normally come in a square block; cut with a knife to make 1cm strips), shirataki noodles; centre: dried egg noodles; bottom, from left: bundles of cellophane noodles (bean vermicelli), dried rice sticks, dried rice vermicelli (bottom).

Persimmon: (also known as the date plum) is thought to be a fruit native to China. The fruit must be very soft and ripe before being eaten or it will have an astringent taste. Peel away skin before eating. ▼

Onions: there are many types of onions available; we used brown onions in our recipes. Other types of related onions shown include, from top: brown, white and purple onions, spring onions (with white bulb) and brown shallots, green shallots (also called spring onions and scallions) chives, garlic chives and dried onion flakes. ▲

Oyster sauce: a rich brown sauce made from oysters cooked in salt and soy sauce, then thickened with different types of starches.

Pappadams: are made from lentils and are sold in packages in several different sizes. Deep or shallow fry them for a few seconds in hot oil; drain on absorbent paper, serve immediately for best results. ▼

Pawpaw: yellow fruit, known in some countries as papaya.

Peppers: (capsicums) we used red or green peppers in this book. ▼

Plain flour: also known as all-purpose flour.

Plum sauce: a dipping sauce which consists of plums preserved in vinegar, sweetened with sugar and flavored with chillies and spices.

Prawns: most of the recipes in this book use green, uncooked prawns. Picture shows how to peel and devein the prawns, and how to "butterfly" them. ▼

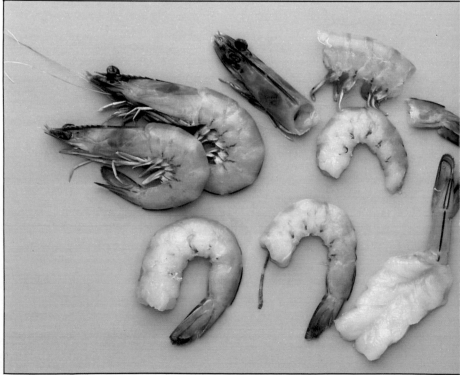

Rice: picture shows some of the ▶ many types of rice available.

There are several ways to cook rice successfully. One method is to bring a large pan of water to the boil, add the rice gradually, boil rapidly, uncovered, for about 10 minutes or until rice is just tender; drain as soon as it is tender. Serve immediately.

If cooking rice in advance, rinse the rice under cold water until it is completely cold. Spread it out on flat tray covered with absorbent paper, or cloth, leave it to dry; store in refrigerator. Rice can be frozen in airtight bags or containers for up to several months without spoiling.

The evaporation method of cooking rice is easy and traditional in Asian countries. Place rice in heavy-based pan, add enough cold water to cover the rice and be about 2cm above the surface of the rice. Cover the pan with a tight-fitting lid. Bring to the boil over a high heat, reduce heat to as low as possible, keep covered, cook for about 20 minutes. Remove from heat, leave covered for a few more minutes to be sure all the water has been completely absorbed by the rice.

Rice can be cooked in a rice cooker which alters the texture and even the taste of the rice. Follow instructions with your appliance, or use the evaporation method as a guide given above. Rice is easy to reheat in a rice cooker.

Rice can be reheated, covered, in a strainer over boiling water. Or in a microwave oven; spread in dish, covered loosely and reheat on HIGH.

ABOVE: From top, left to right: long grain rice, short grain rice, basmati rice, brown rice, Sungold (a partly cooked) rice, glutinous rice, black glutinous rice.

Rockmelon: orange-fleshed fruit, also known as cantaloupe.

Saffron: the most expensive of all spices, is available in threads or ground form. It is made from the dried stamens of the crocus flower.

Sago: (also sold as seed tapioca). Tapioca can be used as a substitute for sago; it will need more cooking. Picture shows from top: tapioca, sago, pearl sago. ◀

Sake: Japan's favorite rice wine, is used in cooking, marinading and as part of dipping sauces. If sake is unavailable, dry sherry, vermouth or brandy can be used as a substitute.

When consumed as a drink, it is served warm; to do this, stand the container in hot water for about 20 minutes to warm the sake.

Sambal oelek: (also spelt sambal ulek) a paste made from ground chillies and salt, can be used as an ingredient or an accompaniment.

Sate sauce: a spicy sauce based on soy sauce; it contains sugar, oil, chilli, onion, garlic and shrimp.

Scallops: We used the scallops with coral (roe) attached throughout this book; they require minimal preparation, see picture. Saucer scallops, found in northern Australian waters, are commonly used in restaurants and are sometimes available in fish markets. They can be substituted in any of these recipes. ▼

Seasoned salt: combine 2 tablespoons coarse kitchen salt with ½ teaspoon five spice powder in heavy-based pan. Stir constantly over low heat for 2 minutes.

Sesame oil: made from roasted, crushed white sesame seeds, is an aromatic golden-colored oil with a nutty flavor. It is always used in small quantities, and added mostly toward the end of the cooking time. It is not the same as the sesame oil sold in health food stores and should not be used to fry food. It is a flavoring only and can be bought in supermarkets and Asian food stores.

Sesame seeds: there are two types, black and white; we used the white variety in this book. They are almost always toasted. See Toasting.

Shallots, brown: see onions.

Shallots, green: see onions.

Shrimp paste: a powerful dark brown flavoring made from salted dried shrimp.

Snake beans: see beans.

Snow peas: (also known as mange tout, sugar peas or Chinese peas) are small flat pods with tiny barely formed peas inside; they are eaten whole — pod and all. Snow peas do need to be topped and tailed, see picture; the older ones also need stringing. They require only a short cooking time (about 30 seconds) either by stir-frying or blanching. ▶

Soy sauce: fermented soy beans are the basis for this extensively used sauce. We used two types of soy sauce in this book, the light and dark variety. The light sauce is generally used with white meat dishes, and the darker variety with red meat dishes but this is only a guide; the dark soy is generally used for color and the light for flavor. We used Soy Superior, the dark variety, and Superior Soy, the light variety. Use Japanese soy sauce in Japanese recipes.

Spinach: (also known as silver beet) is pictured at right and English spinach is pictured below. ▶
   Both are prepared in the same way; remove coarse white stems, cook green leafy parts as individual recipes indicate. ▼

Spring onions: see onions.

Spring roll wrappers or pastry: are sold frozen in Asian food stores in several different sizes. Thaw before using, keep covered with a damp cloth until ready to use.

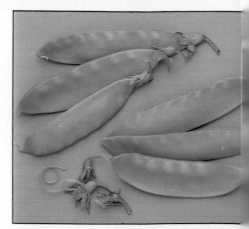

Sprouts: the bean sprouts used in this book are mung bean sprouts; these should be topped and tailed (left). Newly sprouted mung beans are only tiny — about 2.5cm long — and usually have the green outer husk intact (right). These are the simplest beans to sprout at home in a couple of days. There are many varieties of sprouts; they can all be substituted for each other, adjust cooking times to allow for shorter cooking for the finer sprouts like alfalfa. ▼

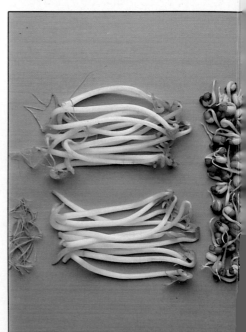

Squid: picture shows the hoods or tubes, rings, and how to cut the diamond pattern into the squid. ▶

Star anise: the dried star-shaped fruit of an evergreen tree. It is used sparingly in Chinese cooking and has an aniseed flavor. ▼

Stock: homemade stock will give you the best flavor in these recipes, however if you want to use stock cubes for convenience, use 1 crumbled stock cube to every 2 cups water. Remember that these cubes contain salt, so allow for this when seasoning the food.

Tamarind sauce: is made from the acid tasting fruit of the tamarind tree. If unavailable, soak about 30g dried tamarind in a cup of water, stand 10 minutes. Squeeze the pulp as dry as possible and use the flavored water. We used Sweet 'n' Tangy Tamarind Sauce made by Sultan's Choice in this book.

Tea: Chinese tea is always made in a china teapot by allowing 2 tablespoons of tea to every 4 cups of boiling water. Brew tea for about 5 minutes, then discard tea, retaining leaves in teapot. Pour on another 4 cups of boiling water and serve. A third brewing retains only partial flavor; never add milk or sugar to Chinese tea, it will spoil the flavor.

Teriyaki sauce: is based on the lighter Japanese soy sauce; it also contains sugar, spices and vinegar.

Toasting: almonds and shredded coconut (right, above) can be toasted in the oven; spread them evenly onto an oven tray, toast in moderate oven for about 5 minutes or until lightly browned. Desiccated coconut and sesame seeds (right) toast more evenly by stirring constantly over heat in a heavy pan; the natural oils will brown both of these ingredients. ▶

Tofu: made from boiled, crushed soy beans to give a type of milk, a coagulant is added, much like the process of cheese making. The curds are then drained and cotton tofu is the result; this is the ordinary tofu (shown at top). Silken tofu (shown at bottom of picture), is undrained and more fragile. Tofu is easily digested, wonderfully nutritious and has a slightly nutty flavor. Make sure you buy it as fresh as possible, keep any leftover tofu in the refrigerator under water, which must be changed daily. ▶

Turmeric: a member of the ginger family, its root is ground and dried, giving the rich yellow powder which gives curry its characteristic color; it is not hot in flavor.

Vinegar: we have specified when to use brown or white malt vinegar; we have also used rice vinegar. This is a colorless vinegar used in cooking and pickling vegetables. This variety is not as sharp as malt vinegar; use cider vinegar as a substitute.

Wasabi: powdered green horseradish used in Japanese cooking. Substitute hot mustard powder or fresh, grated horseradish. It is usually sold in cans and served mixed to a paste with cold water.

Water chestnuts: small white crisp bulbs with a brown skin. Canned water chestnuts are peeled and will keep for about 1 month, covered, in the refrigerator.

White fish: simply means non-oily fish. The variety of fish we used were bream, flathead, whiting, snapper, jewfish and ling.

Wok: a Chinese cooking pan shaped like a large bowl with a rounded base. Flat-based woks are available for electric plates. This wide, open area facilitates quick, even cooking of food.

To season a new wok before cooking, wash well with hot water and liquid detergent to remove any grease, wipe dry. Place wok over heat, add 2 tablespoons oil, 4 chopped green shallots and 1 clove crushed garlic. Swirl mixture over entire surface of wok, place over medium heat for 5 minutes. Discard mixture rinse pan under warm water, wipe dry. Do not scrub wok with any abrasive. Always wash in warm water, then wipe dry; this will protect the wok from rusting. Wipe over inside of wok with a lightly oiled cloth, cover with plastic wrap to prevent dust settling on the surface during storage.

Always heat wok before adding oil, then heat the oil before adding food to prevent food from sticking.

Wonton wrappers: are thin squares or rounds of fresh noodle dough, yellow in color. They are sold frozen; cover with a damp cloth to prevent drying out while using.

Yoghurt: plain, unflavored yoghurt is used extensively in Indian cooking as a tenderiser, enricher, thickener and also as a dessert ingredient.

Zucchini: (also known as courgette and Italian squash) is a member of the marrow family; the average size zucchini we used was about 15cm. ▼

Cup and Spoon Measurements

To ensure accuracy in your recipes use the standard metric measuring equipment approved by Standards Australia:
(a) 250 millilitre cup for measuring liquids. A litre jug *(capacity 4 cups)* is also available.
(b) a graduated set of four cups – measuring 1 cup, half, third and quarter cup – for items such as flour, sugar, etc. When measuring in these fractional cups, level off at the brim.
(c) a graduated set of four spoons: tablespoon *(20 millilitre liquid capacity)*, teaspoon *(5 millilitre)*, half and quarter teaspoons. The Australian, British and American teaspoon each has 5ml capacity.

Approximate cup and spoon conversion chart

Australian	American & British
1 cup	1¼ cups
¾ cup	1 cup
⅔ cup	¾ cup
½ cup	⅔ cup
⅓ cup	½ cup
¼ cup	⅓ cup
2 tablespoons	¼ cup
1 tablespoon	3 teaspoons

Oven Temperatures

Electric	C˙	F˙
Very slow	120	250
Slow	150	300
Moderately slow	160-180	325-350
Moderate	180-200	375-400
Moderately hot	210-230	425-450
Hot	240-250	475-500
Very hot	260	525-550

Gas	C˙	F˙
Very slow	120	250
Slow	150	300
Moderately slow	160	325
Moderate	180	350
Moderately hot	190	375
Hot	200	400
Very hot	230	450

We have used large eggs with an average weight of 60g each in all recipes.
All spoon measurements are level.
Note: NZ, USA and UK all use 15ml tablespoons.

INDEX